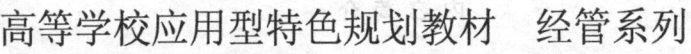

高等学校应用型特色规划教材　经管系列

金融专业英语

主　编　秦　定

副主编　吴　敏　高蓉蓉　马　凌

清华大学出版社

北　京

内容简介

本书是根据普通高等学校应用型特色规划教材编写计划，按照教育部应用型人才培养的教学要求编写的。本书分成国际金融市场、金融机构与运作及金融函电三个部分，用通俗易懂的英语系统地介绍了国际金融市场和金融机构及其运作。本书注重实务操作，并配有与当前经济形势紧密结合的命题对话、专业问答和练习，强化英语在金融领域里的实际运用，从而突出应用型人才培养的特点，培养学生在金融实际工作中运用英语的能力。

本书还结合中国人民银行组织的"金融专业英语证书考试"(Financial English Certificate Test)的内容，着重讲解现代国际金融业务，特别注重训练学生运用英语进行银行业务操作的能力。

本书适合作为大专院校经济和管理及相关专业的教材，同时也可以作为国际贸易和国际金融领域的相关从业人员的参考用书。

本书封面贴有清华大学出版社防伪标签，无标签者不得销售。

版权所有，侵权必究。举报：010-62782989，beiqinquan@tup.tsinghua.edu.cn.

图书在版编目(CIP)数据

金融专业英语/秦定主编；吴敏，高蓉蓉，马凌副主编. —北京：清华大学出版社，2009.6（2025.1重印）
(高等学校应用型特色规划教材　经管系列)
ISBN 978-7-302-20301-8

Ⅰ. ①金…　Ⅱ. ①秦…　②吴…　③高…　④马…　Ⅲ. ①金融—英语—高等学校—教材　Ⅳ. ①H31

中国版本图书馆 CIP 数据核字(2009)第 081111 号

责任编辑：温　洁　汤涌涛
装帧设计：杨玉兰
责任校对：周剑云
责任印制：杨　艳
出版发行：清华大学出版社
　　　　　网　　　址：https://www.tup.com.cn，https://www.wqxuetang.com
　　　　　地　　　址：北京清华大学学研大厦 A 座　　　　邮　　编：100084
　　　　　社 总 机：010-83470000　　　　　　　　　　邮　　购：010-62786544
　　　　　投稿与读者服务：010-62776969，c-service@tup.tsinghua.edu.cn
　　　　　质量反馈：010-62772015，zhiliang@tup.tsinghua.edu.cn
　　　　　课件下载：https://www.tup.com.cn，010-62791865
印 装 者：天津鑫丰华印务有限公司
经　　销：全国新华书店
开　　本：185mm×230mm　　　印　张：15.25　　　字　数：341 千字
版　　次：2009 年 6 月第 1 版　　　　　　　印　次：2025 年 1 月第 14 次印刷
定　　价：42.00 元

产品编号：030414-03

出 版 说 明

　　应用型人才是指能够将专业知识和技能应用于所从事的专业岗位的一种专门人才。应用型人才的本质特征是具有专业基本知识和基本技能，即具有明确的职业性、实用性、实践性和高层次性。加强应用型人才的培养，是"十一五"时期我国教育发展与改革的重要目标，也是协调高等教育规模速度与市场人才需求关系的重要途径。

　　教育部要求今后需要有相当数量的高校致力于培养应用型人才，以满足市场对应用型人才需求量的不断增加。为了培养高素质应用型人才，必须建立完善的教学计划和高水平的课程体系。在教育部有关精神的指导下，我们组织全国高校的专家教授，努力探求更为合理有效的应用型人才培养方案，并结合我国当前的实际情况，编写了这套"高等学校应用型特色规划教材"丛书。

　　为使教材的编写真正切合应用型人才的培养目标，我社编辑在全国范围内走访了大量高等学校，拜访了众多院校主管教学的领导，以及教学一线的系主任和教师，掌握了各地区各学校所设专业的培养目标和办学特色，并广泛、深入地与用人单位进行交流，明确了用人单位的真正需求。这些工作为本套丛书的准确定位、合理选材、突出特色奠定了坚实的基础。

✧ 教材定位

➢ 以就业为导向。在应用型人才培养过程中，充分考虑市场需求，因此本套丛书充分体现"就业导向"的基本思路。

➢ 符合本学科的课程设置要求。以高等教育的培养目标为依据，注重教材的科学性、实用性和通用性。

➢ 定位明确。准确定位教材在人才培养过程中的地位和作用，正确处理教材的读者层次关系，面向就业，突出应用。

➢ 合理选材、编排得当。妥善处理传统内容与现代内容的关系，大力补充新知识、新技术、新工艺和新成果。根据本学科的教学基本要求和教学大纲的要求，制订编写大纲(编写原则、编写特色、编写内容、编写体例等),突出重点、难点。

➤ 建设"立体化"的精品教材体系。提倡教材与电子教案、学习指导、习题解答、课程设计、毕业设计等辅助教学资料配套出版。

✧ 丛书特色

➤ 围绕应用讲理论,突出实践教学环节及特点,包含丰富的案例,并对案例作详细解析,强调实用性和可操作性。

➤ 涉及最新的理论成果和实务案例,充分反映岗位要求,真正体现以就业为导向的培养目标。

➤ 国际化与中国特色相结合,符合高等教育日趋国际化的发展趋势,部分教材采用双语形式。

➤ 在结构的布局、内容重点的选取、案例习题的设计等方面符合教改目标和教学大纲的要求,把教师的备课、授课、辅导答疑等教学环节有机地结合起来。

✧ 读者定位

本系列教材主要面向普通高等院校和高等职业技术院校,适合应用型人才培养的高等院校的教学需要。

✧ 关于作者

丛书编委特聘请执教多年且有较高学术造诣和实践经验的教授参与各册教材的编写,其中有相当一部分的教材主要执笔者是精品课程的负责人,本丛书凝聚了他们多年的教学经验和心血。

✧ 互动交流

本丛书的编写及出版过程,贯穿了清华大学出版社一贯严谨、务实、科学的作风。伴随我国教育改革的不断深入,要编写出满足新形势下教学需求的教材,还需要我们不断地努力、探索和实践。我们真诚希望使用本丛书的教师、学生和其他读者提出宝贵的意见和建议,使之更臻成熟。

清华大学出版社

前　言

在当今全球经济一体化的背景下，中国的经济已逐步地融入世界经济之中。在全球经济一体化这把双刃剑下，中国的经济，尤其是金融业在这场席卷全球的金融危机中，面临着巨大的考验与挑战。面对世界金融市场的动荡，我们应加强对金融业的监管、风险控制和银行治理。因此，我们需要了解世界，需要培养既知晓国际金融专业知识，又精通现代银行业务操作，更能运用英语从事金融业务的复合型人才。但就目前我国的实际情况而言，这方面的人才紧缺，人力资源建设中还存在明显不足，尚有很大的发展空间。

本书正是在这一背景下出版的。全书用英语编写了国际金融市场、金融机构与运作及金融函电三个部分，涉及的内容有国际货币市场、资本市场和外汇市场，商业银行、投资银行与保险公司以及现代银行业务往来函电等。本书注重理论联系实际，紧紧围绕训练和提高金融从业人员和学生的金融英语水平，使其适应日新月异的国际经济形势的要求。本书将帮助读者阅读和理解用英语撰写的金融专业文章，了解金融知识，掌握基本的业务原理和一般的业务程序，并能用英语撰写银行业务函电和业务文件，同时还会用英语来交流金融专业的话题。

本书主要体现“实”和“新”两大特点。“实”，本书立足于金融专业的实用性，通过命题对话、专业问答等形式给金融从业人员和学生提供一个英语专业口语训练的机会，帮助读者和学生掌握金融实务操作中常用的英语词句并能快速上手。本书配有阅读理解、单项选择、填空和翻译等练习，可为从事金融工作的读者和金融专业的学生日后参加中国人民银行举办的“金融专业英语证书考试”打下良好的基础。本书的另一个特点是“新”，作者着眼于较高的立意，导入近年来金融领域里的一些新发展，对传统业务进行补充和完善，让读者在学习金融英语的同时也了解一些金融业的前沿动态。

本书的实践性较强，它以简单实用、前沿全面的特色适应市场需求。本书可用作高等院校金融专业学生的教材，也可作为正在或有志于从事金融业的人员的参考用书。

本书总体框架和大纲由秦定负责设计，内容和练习由秦定拟定和编写，吴敏、高蓉蓉和马凌负责编写和翻译了一些章节的内容，最后由秦定对全书进行统稿。

感谢清华大学出版社对本教材编写的鼎力支持和热情帮助，在此表示由衷的敬意和感谢。

在本书的编写过程中，参阅、吸收和借鉴了国内外专家学者有关的文献，在此深表感谢。

因编者水平有限，书中难免存在不足和遗漏，敬请读者批评指正。

编　者

目　录

Part Ⅰ　Financial Markets

Chapter 1　Functions of Financial Markets 3

1.1　Significance 3

1.2　Functions 4

参考译文 7

Subject Topic(命题对话) 10

Questions and Answers(专业问答) 11

Exercises(练习) 12

Chapter 2　Money Markets 18

2.1　Characteristics 18

2.2　Participants of Money Market 19

2.3　Instruments of Money Market 21

参考译文 24

Subject Topic(命题对话) 28

Questions and Answers(专业问答) 30

Exercises(练习) 30

Chapter 3　Capital Markets 33

3.1　Purpose and Participants..33

3.2　Trading in the Capital Market 34

参考译文 36

Subject Topic(命题对话) 39

Questions and Answers(专业问答) 41

Exercises(练习) 42

Chapter 4　Foreign Exchange Markets 49

4.1　Meanings of Foreign Exchange 49

4.2　Financial Derivatives 53

4.3　Exchange Control 58

参考译文 60

Subject Topic(命题对话) 68

Questions and Answers(专业问答) 71

Exercises(练习) 72

Part Ⅱ　Financial Institutions and Their Operations

Chapter 5　Commercial Banking 81

5.1　Intermediary Services 81

5.2　International Settlement 83

5.3　Credit Loan 95

参考译文 106

Subject Topic(命题对话) 127

Questions and Answers(专业问答) 128

Exercises(练习) 129

Chapter 6　Investment Banking 149

6.1　Investment Banking 149

6.2　Backgrounds 149

6.3　Investment Banks and Financial System 151

6.4　Investment Banking Activities 152

6.5　Prospect of Investment Banking 153

参考译文 154

Subject Topic(命题对话) 158

Questions and Answers(专业问答) 159

Exercises(练习) 159

Chapter 7　Insurance 161

7.1　What Is Insurance and How It Works? 161

7.2　The Types of Insurance 163

7.3　The Fundamentals of Insurance 163

7.4　Legal Principles of Insurance 165

7.5　Insurance Market 167

参考译文 169

Subject Topic(命题对话) 176

Questions and Answers(专业问答) 177

Exercises(练习) 178

Chapter 8　Securities 182

8.1　The Types of Securities 182

8.2　Securities Market 186

8.3　Securities Investment 188

参考译文 192

Subject Topic(命题对话) 199

Questions and Answers(专业问答) 201

Exercises(练习) 202

Part Ⅲ　Financial Communications

Chapter 9　Banking Communications on Remittance and Collections 207

9.1　Mail Transfer 207

9.2　Demand Draft 207

9.3　Telegraphic Transfer 208

9.4　Accounts Intercourse 208

9.5　Letters on Collections 211

Chapter 10　Banking Communications on Letter of Credit 213

10.1　Letters between Banks 213

10.2　Letters on Credit Operations 214

Chapter 11　Correspondent Banking 220

11.1　Terms and Conditions 220

11.2　Signature Books and Test Keys 220

Chapter 12　Credit Inquiry 222

12.1　Credit Inquiry on Companies 222

12.2　Credit Inquiry on Individuals 223

Key to Exercises 224

参考文献 232

Part I Financial Markets

- Chapter 1 Functions of Financial Markets
- Chapter 2 Money Markets
- Chapter 3 Capital Markets
- Chapter 4 Foreign Exchange Markets

Chapter 1

Functions of Financial Markets

1.1 Significance

The word "finance" signifies capital in monetary form, that is, in the form of funds lent or borrowed, normally for capital purposes, through financial markets or financial institutions. When finance goes international, it is then an international finance.

What is a financial market? It is a place where financial transactions take place. Financial markets facilitate the lending of funds from savers to those who wish to undertake investments. Those that wish to borrow to finance investment projects sell financial instruments to savers.

When an investor purchases the securities issued by ultimate borrowers (those who use the funds to invest in real assets), capital market operations for equities, bonds would fall largely into this category. When an investor chooses to invest in the obligations of financial intermediaries, which in turn lend the funds to those who invest in real assets, they are operations in money market for term deposits and loans, interbank transactions of such nature. The primary distinction between the two channels is that, in the first case, i.e. direct financing, the investor is faced directly with the credit risk of the issuer, while in the second case, i.e. financing through financial intermediation, a financial institution, such as a bank, interjects itself between users and providers of funds. Any analysis of the sector of money market dominated by financial intermediaries must be very much concerned with these financial institutions themselves (their policies, financial conditions and official regulatory environment) in addition to those factors governing the suppliers and users of funds.

International financial transactions include purchases and sales of foreign currency, securities, gold bullion, and lending and borrowing.

Foreign exchange marker deals with the exchanges of different means of payment. These exchanges are necessary for international capital flows. As the relative values among different currencies (the exchange rates) will fluctuate according to economic and political circumstances of the currencies of the relative countries, international investors or financiers face exchange risks. To this end, foreign exchange markets provide services, such as forward transactions and foreign currency futures to eliminate such risks.

1.2　Functions

Apart from borrowing from banks, a firm or an individual can obtain funds in a financial market in two ways. The most common method is to issue a debt instrument, such as a bond or a mortgage, which is a contractual agreement by the borrower to pay the holder of the instrument fixed amounts at regular intervals (interest and principal payments) until a specified date (the maturity date), when a final payment is made. The maturity of a debt instrument is short-term if its maturity is less than a year and long-term if its maturity is ten years or long. Debt instruments with a maturity between one and ten years are said to be intermediate-term.

The second method of raising funds is by issuing equities, such as common stock, which are claim to share in the net income (income after expenses and taxes) and the assets of a business. Equities usually earn periodic payment (dividends) and are considered long-term securities because they have no maturity date.

A primary market is a financial market in which new issues of a security,

Chapter 1　Functions of Financial Markets

such as a bond or a stock, are sold to initial buyers by the corporation or government agency borrowing the funds. A secondary market is a financial market in which securities that have been previously issued (and are thus secondhand) can be resold.

The primary market for securities is not well known to the public because the selling of securities to initial buyers take place behind doors. An important financial instrument that assists in the initial sale of securities in the primary market is the investment bank. It does this by underwriting securities, that is, it guarantees a price for a corporation's securities and then sells them to the public.

When an individual buys a security in the secondary market, the person who sold the security receives money in exchange for the security, but the corporation that issued the security acquires no new funds. A corporation acquires new funds only when its security are first sold in the primary market. Nonetheless, the secondary market serves two important functions. First, financial instruments are more liquid. The increased liquidity of the instruments makes them more desirable and thus easier for the issuing firm to sell in the primary market. Second, they determine the price of the security that the issuing firm sells in the primary market. The firms that buy securities in the primary market will pay the issuing corporation no more than the price that they think the secondary market will set for this security. The higher the security's price in the secondary market, the higher the price that the issuing firm will receive for a security in the primary market and hence the greater the amount of capital it can raise. Conditions in the secondary market are therefore the most relevant to corporations issuing securities. It is for this reason that studies dealing with financial market focus the behavior of secondary markets rather than primary markets.

Another way of distinguishing market is on the basis of the maturity of the securities traded in each market. The money market is a financial market in which only short-term debt instruments (maturity of less one year) are traded; the capital market is the market in which long-term debt (maturity of one year or longer) and equity instruments are traded. Money market securities are usually more widely traded than long-term securities and so they are more liquid. In addition, short-term securities have smaller fluctuations in prices than long-term securities, making them the safer investment. As a result, corporations and banks actively use this market to earn interest on surplus funds that they expect to have only temporarily. Capital market securities, such as stocks and long-term bonds, are often held by individuals and financial intermediaries such as insurance companies and pension funds, which have little uncertainty about the amount of funds they will have available in the future.

参考译文

第 I 部分　金融市场

第1章　金融市场的作用

1.1　含义

"金融"即货币资金的融通和交易，是指货币资金通过金融市场或金融机构进行借贷和交易。当资金的融通在国际间进行时，即为国际金融。

什么是金融市场？金融市场即金融交易的场所，它为资金余缺方提供融资便利，创造各种金融工具供人们选择。

当投资者购买了最终借款人(借款人用所筹资金投资实业)发行的证券，这些证券再通过资本市场运作，股票、债券可以归为这一类。当投资者选择投资金融中介机构的债务，再由金融中介机构把所筹资金贷给实际资金需求方，这是通过货币市场以存款和贷款的形式运作。这两种融资渠道的根本区别在于：第一种渠道是直接融资，投资者直接承担发行人的信贷风险；第二种渠道是间接融资，资金有余方和资金不足方的融通是通过金融中介或机构进行的，比如银行作为资金使用方和资金提供方的中介。对以金融中介机构为主导的货币市场部门的分析除了与影响资金供求方的因素有关外，还与这些金融机构本身(他们的政策和财务状况及政府的监管环境)密切相关。

国际金融市场的交易包括外汇、证券、黄金的买卖以及资金的借贷。

外汇交易商从事不同货币之间的兑换，这些兑换促进了国际间的资金流动。因为不同货币的相对价值(即汇率)会因一国或地区的经济、政治状况而发生波动，国际投资者或金融家会因此面临汇率风险。为此，外汇市场提供如远期交易和外汇期货等工具来消除此类风险。

1.2 作用

除了从银行借款，企业或个人还可以通过两种途径从金融市场获取资金。最常见的方法是发行债务工具，如债券或抵押。债券是借款人向债权人出具的合约，合约规定借款人必须按期还本付息，直到某一特定日期(到期日)付款完毕。如果债券的期限在 1 年以内，则称为短期债券；期限在 10 年以上称为长期债券；期限在 1～10 年称为中期债券。

第二种方法是通过发行股票筹集资金，如普通股股票，普通股享有净利润(又称净收益，收入减去支出和税收)的索取权和剩余财产的清偿权。股票一般会定期获得收益(即股息)，因为没有到期日，股票被看作一种长期证券。

初级市场(又称证券发行市场、一级市场)是发行新证券(如债券和股票)的金融市场，公司或政府机构通过初级市场把证券出售给初始投资者筹集资金。二级市场(又称证券交易市场、次级市场)是已发行证券买卖或转让的市场。

初级市场发行的证券并不为公众所熟悉，因为证券的出售并不被初始投资者所知。投资银行是帮助新证券在一级市场销售的重要角色。投资银行进行证券的承销，保证按协定价格购入公司发行的证券，再把它们出售给公众。

个人投资者在二级市场购买证券后，证券的出售方便获得了资金，但发行证券的公司并没有得到新的资金。公司只有在初级市场上首次发行证券时才能获得新的资金来源。尽管如此，二级市场有两个重要的功能。第一个功能是增强了金融工具的流动性。流动性的增强使得这些金融工具更受人欢迎，也有利于公司在初级市场上发行证券。第二个功能是二级市场决定了证券发行公司在一级市场出售证券的价格。在初级市场承销证券的公司不会以超过二级市场能出售的价格支付给发行证券的公司。二级市场上证券的价格越高，在初级市场上发行证券的公司出售证券的价格也越高，从而能筹集更多的资金。二级市场的行情直接影响到公司证券的发行。正

Chapter 1 Functions of Financial Markets

是因为这个原因，很多关于金融市场的研究把重点放在二级市场的行为而非一级市场。

另外一种区分市场的方法是根据市场交易对象的期限来划分的。货币市场是指期限在一年以内的短期金融工具交易的市场；资本市场是指期限在一年以上的的长期金融工具交易的市场。与长期证券相比较，货币市场证券的买卖通常更广泛，因而流动性更强。另外，短期证券相对于长期证券价格波动较小，也更安全。因此，公司和银行常常把它们的闲置资金投放在货币市场获得利息。股票和长期债券等资本市场证券常常被个人和金融中介机构(如保险公司和养老基金)持有，因为他们未来获得资金的不确定性较小。

Subject Topic(命题对话)

Global Economic Integration
(全球经济一体化)

A: What are the signs of global economic integration?

B: I think global economic integration is an inevitable trend for the future. The interaction and inter-reliance of the world economy has been greatly strengthened. The founding of the World Trade Organization has speed up economic globalization. Markets in different areas have become linked closely together. They have been gradually integration into one single market. In addition, the development of regional economic integration such as the EU and APEC have made great contributions to global economic integration because they have set up models for other countries in the world to follow.

A: Let's go into some details about global economic integration. What I am interested is the global financial arena. As we know, frequent and fierce mergers and acquisitions are now happening in the global financial area. What are the reasons for that?

B: Well, I think governments' relaxation of control is the major factor that stimulates mergers and buyouts. In 1994, the U.S. government relieved its ban on banks' cross-state operation and permitted commercial banks to engage in security transaction. As a result, nearly 1000 banks enlarged their scale through merger in 1996.

The second reason is that mergers among financial institutions will achieve optimum allocation of financial resources so that banks will increase their profits. Through merger, the average capital turnover ratio of commercial banks in the U.S. hit 1.2% in 1996.

Mergers among financial institutions will help banks to realize scale

Chapter 1　Functions of Financial Markets

operation and increase their resistance to risks. In addition, in this way, financial institutions that were engaged in some specific areas before will now be able to provide comprehensive services to customers.

The last reason is that financial institutions can increase their economic power to meet the coming challenges in the international financial area. In the 1990s, the U.S. commercial banks beat their competitors in Japan and took the leading role in the international banking industry because of mergers.

Questions and Answers(专业问答)

1. What is the international balance of payment and which items does it constitute by?

    —The balance of payment is a statement of a country's monetary transactions with the rest of the world. They are current account, capital account and balance item.

2. Which methods could be used to balance the international payment deficit?

    —The methods will be used as following:

    a. import restriction

    b. export promotion

    c. tighten monetary policy

    d. tighten fiscal policy

    e. devaluation

3. Which categories do financial markets mainly include?

    —They include foreign exchange market, money market, capital market and gold market.

11

4. What are the major functions of modern commercial bank?

a. They are medium of credit.

b. They are medium of payment.

c. They change money into capital.

d. They are creation of credit.

Exercises(练习)

Reading Comprehension

Passage One

The London Markets

For centuries prior to the 1930s London maintained its preeminence as an international financial center. It does not matter that Britain no longer has the economic, political, and military prosperous that it once had. London still is unparalleled in the variety of services and the degree of financial expertise that it possesses, and London continues, despite all of the weakness of the British economy, to be a very dynamic and powerful financial market. Especially important is its role as an "offshore" financial center.

1. For centuries prior to the 1930s London had the economic, political and military preeminence.

   A. Right   B. Wrong   C. Doesn't say

2. Because of the weakness of the British economy, London is no longer the international financial center.

   A. Right   B. Wrong   C. Doesn't say

3. Foreign markets which will accept the deposit and lending of foreign currencies have a very long history.

   A. Right   B. Wrong   C. Doesn't say

Chapter 1 Functions of Financial Markets

Passage Two

The U.S. Markets

In the aftermath of the Second World War, here was absolutely no doubt as to where the financial leadership of the world had moved. The dollar had become the preferred currency for international trade and investment (supplanting the pound sterling for the first time in history). The U.S. economy was the only major economy that had survived the war not only in good condition but in far stronger condition than it had been at the start of the war. The United States was the only country which could supply much of the goods that reconstruction demanded. The U.S. financial markets were the only markets that had the needed financial resources. Thus, for many years the domestic U.S. financial markets were avidly used by foreign, corporate, and governmental borrowers to help finance their reconstruction and expansionary needs.

The U.S. dollar was, at the same time, the only major freely convertible currency. Until 1958 even the major Western European currencies were inconvertible to various extents. Coupled with this was a wide range of laws which restricted foreign access to most of those markets. The domestic U.S. markets were the obvious alternative.

1. After World War 2, the financial leadership of the world moved to the United States.

    A. Right   B. Wrong   C. Doesn't say

2. After the 1930s, London continued to keep its preeminence as the financial center.

    A. Right   B. Wrong   C. Doesn't say

3. Before 1958, the U.S. dollar was the only convertible currency.

    A. Right   B. Wrong   C. Doesn't say

13

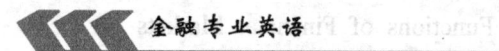

Passage Three

International Financial Markets

International financial markets comprise all of those markets where either the placer or taker of funds is from a country outside of the market being utilized. For example, for almost two centuries London was the site of the major market for foreign borrowers either to obtain bank loans or to sell their bonds; such funds were provided in pounds sterling. Much of the early industrial development in the United States, including a major share of American railroads, was financed with funds from London. Even the governments of individual states and the U.S. government itself utilized the British markets.

Correspondingly, international financial markets exist for the investors when they elect to invest their funds in a financial market outside of their home country. The Egyptian exporter who choose to deposit his U.S. dollar receipts in New York or London is a participant in such a market.

Not too surprisingly, the markets which tend to attract deposits from abroad also tend to be markets which provide funds abroad—rather a symmetrical relationship. This will be seen to be true for most of the markets which will be examined here, whether local funds are used for financing foreign needs (as was commonly true of the aforementioned British financing in the 19th century)or whether the funds "flow through" from one country to another.

International financial markets can develop anywhere—so long as the local government permits such activity and so long as the potential users are attracted to the market. Many governments discourage such activity. Other governments favor the internationalization of their markets but unable to attract the business. For example, political unrest or poor communications facilities(e.g., Egypt) can prevent the development of international money and capital markets in those countries or even (as in the case of Lebanon) comprise.

1. What do the international financial markets comprise?

Chapter 1　Functions of Financial Markets

A. The international financial markets comprise four markets.

B. The international financial markets comprise gold market and money market.

C. The international financial markets comprise capital market and money market.

D. The international financial markets comprise gold market and foreign exchange market.

2.　What are the factors that affect the development of international financial markets?

A. government intervention　　　B. political situation

C. communications facilities　　　D. All of the above

3.　How long is the history of international financial markets?

A. International financial markets have existed for 100 years.

B. International financial markets have existed for hundreds of years.

C. International financial markets have existed for 80 years.

D. International financial markets have existed for 50 years.

Multiple Choice

1.　Special Drawing Rights(SDRs) is a type of international money that was first created in_____.

A. 1948　　　B. 1965　　　C. 1969　　　D. 1972

2.　A foreign branch is _____.

A. a banking office in a foreign country

B. a separate entity engaging in international business

C. a representative office

D. a kind of correspondent

3.　A deficit in the balance of payments can be accommodated by _____.

A. drawing on the reserves

B. importing from other countries

C. making money

D. exporting to other countries

4. _____markets are those which are concerned with the raising of new financial claims. _____markets are those which are concerned with the buying and selling second-hand of existing financial claims.

A. Primary…Secondary

B. Secondary…Primary

C. First…Second

D. Second…First

Cloze Test

Credit risk ___1___ the ability of an entity to repay its ___2___, country risk to the ability and willingness of borrowers within a country to meet their ___3___. Risk sharing arrangements ___4___ banks to spread loan risks, avoid too much exposure to individual borrowers and accordingly undertake ___5___ to a wider range of entities than they would consider prudent to do individually. Syndicates ___6___ loan risks in formal and identifiable ways, making explicit each bank's contribution ___7___ the total risk. Interbank markets do so in less formal ways, ___8___ we have noted above. ___9___ that multilateral development banks and official institutions co-finance with banks or guarantee bank loans, the risk to commercial banks is partly underwritten. Finally, "cross default" clauses in syndication contracts give any bank the right to accelerate a loan should the borrower ___10___ on any other loan. These various arrangements were developed and legally refined so that banks undertaking international lending would be largely protected from the risks that participating banks would otherwise face.

1. A. refer to   B. refers to

   C. is referred to as   D. refers as

2. A. obligation   B. obligations

Chapter 1   Functions of Financial Markets

C. money

D. debts

3. A. rights

B. right

C. obligations

D. obligation

4. A. adopt to

B. are adopted by

C. adopted by

D. adopt by

5. A. lending

B. lendings

C. borrowing

D. borrowings

6. A. divide

B. divide into

C. divide up

D. divide on

7. A. to   B. in   C. on   D. by

8. A. before   B. or   C. so that   D. as

9. A. Within the extent   B. Above the extent

   C. Below the extent   D. To the extent

10. A. default   B. fault

    C. error   D. object

17

Chapter 2

Money Markets

2.1 Characteristics

It is no wonder that businesses have aggressively pursued alternatives to low-interest-rate bank accounts. One such alternative is provided by the money markets. This chapter carefully reviews the money markets and the instruments that are traded there. In addition, we discuss why the money markets are important to our financial system.

Money market instruments, which are discussed in detail later in this chapter, have three basic characteristics in common:

- They are usually sold in large denominations.
- They have low default risk.
- They mature in one year or less from their original issue date. Most money market instruments mature in less than 120 days.

The well-developed secondary market for money market instruments makes the money market an ideal place for a firm or financial institution to "warehouse" surplus funds for short periods of time until they are needed. Similarly, the money market provide a low-cost source of the funds to firms, the government, and intermediaries that need a short-term infusion of funds.

Most investors in the money market who are temporarily warehousing funds are ordinarily not trying to earn unusually high returns on their money market funds. Rather, they use the money market as an interim investment that provides a higher return than holding cash or money in banks. They may feel

Chapter 2   Money Markets

that market conditions are not right to warrant the purchase of additional stock, or they may expect interest rates to rise and hence not want to purchase bonds. Idle cash represents an opportunity cost in terms of lost interest income. The money markets provide means to invest idle funds and to reduce this opportunity cost. At the same time, the sellers of money market instruments find that the money market provide a low-cost source of temporary funds.

Why do corporations and the government sometimes need to get their hands on funds quickly? The primary reason is that cash inflows and outflows are rarely synchronized. Government tax revenues, for example, usually come only at certain time of the year, but expenses are incurred all year long. The government can borrow short-term funds that it will pay back when it receives tax revenues. Businesses also face the problems caused by revenues and expenses occurring at different times. The money market provides an efficient, low-cost way of solving these problems.

2.2   Participants of Money Market

1. The Government

In money market, the government is unique because it is always a supplier and demander of money market funds. The U.S. Treasury is the largest of all money market borrowers worldwide. It issues Treasury bills (often called T-bills) and other securities that are popular with other money market participants. Short-term issues enable the government to raise the maturing issues.

2. The Central Bank

The Central Bank is the Treasury's agent for the distribution of government securities. The central bank holds vast quantities of Treasury securities that it sells if it believes that the money supply should be reduced. Similarly, the central bank purchases Treasury securities if it believes that the money supply

19

should be expanded. The central bank's responsibility for the money supply makes it the single most influential participant in the money market.

3. Commercial Banks

Commercial banks hold a larger percentage of government securities than any other group of financial institutions. This is partly because of regulations that limit the investment opportunities available to banks. Specifically, banks are prohibited from owning risky securities, such as stocks or corporate bonds. There are no restrictions against holding Treasury securities because of their low risk and high liquidity.

Banks are also the major issuer of negotiable certificates of deposit (CDs), banker's acceptances, and repurchase agreements. In addition to money market securities to help manage their own liquidity, many banks trade on behalf of their customers.

Not all commercial banks deal for their customers in the secondary money market. The ones that do are among the largest in the country and are often referred to as money center banks.

4. Businesses

Many businesses buy and sell securities in the money market. Such activity is usually limited to major corporations because of the large transactions involved. As discussed earlier, the money market is used extensively by businesses both to warehouse surplus funds and to raise short-term funds.

5. Investment Companies

Large diversified brokerage firms are active in money markets. The primary function of these dealers is to "make a market" for money market securities by maintaining an inventory from which to buy or sell. These firms are very important to the liquidity of the money market because they help ensure that both buyers and sellers can readily market their securities in the primary market as well as in the secondary market.

6. Insurance Companies

Property and casualty insurance companies must maintain liquidity because of their unpredictable need for funds. To meet this demand, the insurance companies sell some of their money market securities to raise cash.

As to the life insurance companies, because their obligations are reasonably predictable, large money market security holdings are unnecessary. However, it is a common practice that an individual can have his/her money invested in the money market through the agent department of banks and investment companies, to earn a higher interest rate than otherwise deposited in the banks.

2.3　Instruments of Money Market

Securities with maturities within one year are referred to as money market instruments. A variety of money market instruments are available to meet the diverse needs of market participants. The more popular money market instruments are:

- Treasury bills
- Inter-bank markets
- Commercial paper
- Negotiable certificates of deposit
- Banker's acceptances

1. Treasury Bills

To financial the national debt, the government issues a variety of debt securities. The most widely held liquid security is the Treasury bill, which is commonly issued by the ministry of finance. However, some Treasury bills, like the Treasury bill of the U. S. government, do not actually pay interest. Instead

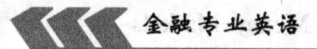

they are issued at a discount from par (their value at maturity). The investor's yield comes from the increase in the value of the security between the time it was purchased and the time it matures.

2. Inter-bank Markets

Inter-bank markets are money markets in which short-term funds transferred (loaned or borrowed) between financial institutions, usually for a period of one day, that is, they are usually overnight investment. The interest rate for borrowing these funds is close to, but always slightly higher than rate that is available from the central bank.

3. Commercial Paper

Commercial paper is a short term debt instrument issued only by well-known, larger and creditworthy corporations. It is typically unsecured, and the interest rate placed on it reflects the firm's level of risk. It is normally issued to provide liquidity or finance a firm's investment and accounts receivable. The issuance of commercial paper is an alternative to short-term bank loan.

4. NCDs or CDs

A negotiable certificate of deposit is a bank-issued security that documents a deposit and specifies the interest rate and the maturity date. It was firstly issued in 1961 by Citibank. Because a maturity date is specified, a CD is a term security as opposed to a demand deposit. Term securities have a specified maturity date while demand deposits can be withdrawn at any time. A CD is also called a bearer instrument. This means that whoever holds the instrument at maturity receives the principal and interest. The CD can be bought and sold until maturity.

Chapter 2 Money Markets

5. Bank's Acceptances

A bank's acceptance is an order to pay a specified amount of money to the bearer on a given date. Banker's acceptances have been in use since the twelfth century, and are commonly used for international trade transactions.

参考译文

第2章 货币市场

2.1 货币市场的特征

毫无疑问，企业一直都在积极地寻求能够替代低利率银行账户的其他金融工具。货币市场为企业提供了一种选择。这一章详细介绍货币市场以及货币市场的交易工具。此外，还会讨论货币市场对于金融体系的重要性。

本章后文要讨论的货币市场工具一般具有三个基本特征：

● 金额大；

● 低违约风险；

● 发行日到到期日的期限在一年或一年以下。大部分货币市场工具的期限小于120天。

二级市场的良好发展使货币市场成为企业或金融机构短期存放闲置资金的理想场所，直到他们需要这些资金为止。同时，货币市场为企业、政府和那些需要短期资金注入的中介机构提供了低成本的资金来源。

大多数把闲置资金临时存放在货币市场上的投资者并不试图获得非常高的收益。相反，他们利用货币市场进行临时投资是因为其收益比持有现金或银行存款更高。他们可能认为，市场条件不值得购买更多的股票，或者他们可能希望利率上升，因此不想购买债券。闲置现金的机会成本是损失的利息收入。货币市场为闲置资金提供金融工具进行投资来减少其机会成本。与此同时，货币市场金融工具的卖方(资金的需求方)可以利用货币市场筹措低成本的临时性资金。

为什么公司和政府有时需要迅速把资金弄到手？主要的原因是现金的流入和流出很少同步。例如，政府的税收收入，常常在一年中固定的时间获得，但是政府支出一年中每天都有。政府可以借用短期资金，在他收到税收时进行偿还。企业也会因为收入和支出的期限不同而面临同样的问题。

货币市场提供了一个有效的，低成本的方式来解决这些问题。

2.2 货币市场的参与者

1. 政府

在货币市场上，政府是独一无二的，因为他既是资金的需求方，又是资金的供给方。美国财政部是世界货币市场上最大的借款者。美国财政部发行的国库券(英文简称 T-bill)和其他债券受到货币市场参与者的追捧。短期证券发行能使政府筹集将要到期的证券。

2. 中央银行

中央银行作为财政部的代理人销售政府债券。中央银行持有大量政府债券。如果央行认为市场上货币供应量应减少，就会出售债券；同样，如果它认为货币供应量应该增加，就会购买政府债券。央行维持货币供应量稳定的职责使它成为货币市场中一个最有影响力的参与者。

3. 商业银行

商业银行持有的政府债券的比例要高于其他金融机构。这部分是由于相关法规限制了商业银行的投资机会。具体来说，商业银行被禁止持有股票或企业债券等高风险的证券，而由于政府债券的低风险和高流动性，商业银行持有政府债券没有任何限制。

商业银行还是可转让定期存单、银行承兑汇票和回购协议的主要发行者。银行除了利用货币市场交易来管理其流动性，还可以代表他们的客户进行交易。

并不是所有的商业银行都代表他们的客户在二级货币市场进行交易。能够代表客户去交易的通常是一个国家最大的商业银行，通常被指定为货币中心银行。

4. 商业企业

许多企业在货币市场上买卖证券。因为交易涉及的金额较大，这种活动通常仅限于大型企业。如前所述，货币市场可以被企业用来放置闲置资金，也可以用来筹集闲置资金。

5. 投资公司

货币市场也活跃着大量形形色色的经纪公司。这些经纪公司(做市商)的主要职能是"做市"，即为买卖双方持有一些货币市场证券的存货。这些公司对维持货币市场的流动性非常重要，因为它们有助于确保买卖双方很容易在初级市场和二级市场上推销其证券。

6. 保险公司

财产和人身意外伤害保险的公司必须保持流动性，因为他们无法预测何时需要资金。为了满足这种需求，保险公司出售他们的一些货币市场证券，以筹集资金。

至于寿险公司，他们的资金需求是可预期的，因而没有必要大量持有货币市场证券。然而，一种常见的做法是，个人可以通过银行和投资公司代理部门把他/她的钱投资于货币市场，以赚取比把钱存放在银行所获利息更高的利息。

2.3 货币市场工具

期限在一年内的证券被称为货币市场工具。各种货币市场工具可用来满足市场参与者的各种不同需求。较受欢迎的货币市场工具是：

- 国库券
- 银行同业拆借市场
- 商业票据
- 可转让定期存单
- 银行承兑票据

1. 国库券

政府发行各种各样的债务证券为政府的债务融资。最为广泛持有的流动性债券是国库券，通常由财政部发行。然而，一些国库券(如美国政府的国库券)并不支付利息。相反，它们通常折价发行。投资者获得的收益即证券购买价格与到期价格的差额。

2. 银行同业拆借市场

银行同业拆借市场是短期资金在金融机构间转移(借贷)的市场，同业拆借的期限一般为 1 天或隔夜。同业拆借市场的利率接近于但总是略高于从中央银行借款的利率。

3. 商业票据

商业票据是一种短期债务工具，只有著名的、较大的和信誉良好的企业才有资格发行。它通常是无担保的，利率反映了票据发行公司的风险水平。商业票据的发行通常是为了解决流动性或者为公司的投资和应收账款融资。商业票据的发行是除银行短期贷款之外的另一种融资选择。

4. 可转让定期存单

可转让定期存单是一种由银行发行，指定利率和到期日，可以在市场上转让的存款单据。最早由花旗银行于1961年发行。由于指定到期日期，可转让定期存单是一种定期存款，而不是活期存款。定期存款有一个指定的到期日，而活期存款可随时提取。可转让定期存单也可称为不记名存单，这意味着谁持有票据，谁就可以在到期时获得本金和利息。在到期前可转让定期存单可以自由买卖。

5. 银行承兑

银行承兑是在约定的日期支付给持票人一定金额的支付命令。银行承兑自12世纪就已开始使用，是国际贸易中一种常用的工具。

Subject Topic(命题对话)

Central Bank

(中央银行)

A: What is a central bank?

B: A central bank is a government agency in charge of a country's finance. It controls the credit activities of financial institutions by making relevant policies, rules and regulations. A central bank restricts the credit scale of commercial banks with monetary tools. At the same time a central bank also has the characteristics of an ordinary bank. For example, it also engages in some credit and clearing operations.

A: What are the functions of a central bank?

B: Basically, a central bank performs three main functions. Firstly, it is the only bank that can issue currency in a country. Secondly, it is called "the government bank." A central bank makes and carries out monetary policies and regulates all financial activities in a country. Finally, a central bank is also called "the banks' bank" because it is the lender of last resort to commercial banks.

A: Which bank is the central bank in China?

B: The People's Bank of China is the central bank of China.

A: In order to establish a modern financial system, the government has taken reforming the management of the central bank as a priority. The People's Bank of China will close all the provincial branches and set up the so-called "trans-administrative regional banks". The purpose of this is to enhance its independence and authority in supervision. What do you think might be the significance of this move?

B: The establishment of trans-administrative regional banks will help to

Chapter 2　Money Markets

maintain the central bank's independence. Interference from local governments can be avoided. Such interference would probably lead to excessive of currency and inflation.

A: The establishment of such banks should also improve the development of the regions where they are located. Therefore, we can promote the coordination of the national economy.

B: All in all, it is a key step in the financial reform to perfect our socialist market-oriented financial system. In order to reform the financial system, the central bank will encourage mergers between banks on the provincial and city level, and cut down the number of branches with heavy losses. Moreover, the central bank will organize commercial banks to establish a multi-level financial system.

A: This year, the People's Bank of China has gradually turned its direct macro-economic control system into an indirect control system. What exactly did the central bank do?

B: Right. There were three steps. From the 1st of January, the central bank replaced the credit line system with the asset-liability management system. This was a very important measure. With the abolition of the basic credit line, commercial banks will obtain more independence in their operation. They will obtain more freedom to determine their credit scale and to provide more financial support for state-owned enterprises. This new measure will also optimize the asset and liability structure of commercial banks and improve their operation efficiency.

A: As far as the central bank is concerned, the abolition of the basic credit line shows that the central bank has achieve great progress in its approach to the indirect control over commercial banks.

B: The second step was to reform the reserve requirement policy. The central bank canceled the reserve fund account and reduced the reserve requirement system as a monetary policy tool.

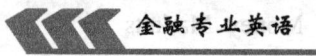

A: I think it will also decrease the interest burden of commercial banks because they will no longer have to depend too much on the central bank for loans.

B: The third step was that the central bank has reduced interest rates three times this year in order to regulate the macro economy.

Questions and Answers(专业问答)

1. What is Capital Adequacy Ratio?

    —Capital Adequacy Ratio is the ratio of the total capital base to the total risk weighted assets.

2. Which two forms are there of inflation?

    —They are demand-full inflation and cost-push inflation.

3. What are the functions of a central bank?

    —It is :

    a. Banker to the government.

    b. Banker to the commercial banks.

    c. Lender of last resort.

Exercises(练习)

Reading Comprehension

Passage One

Market risk can be further divided into exchange rate risk and interest rate risk.

Banks face a risk of losses in positions arising from movements in exchange rates. Established accounting principals cause these risks to be typically most visible in a bank's trading activities. Banks act as "market makers" in foreign exchange markets by quoting rates to their customers and by

Chapter 2 Money Markets

taking open positions in foreign currencies. The risk inherent in foreign exchange business, particularly in running open foreign exchange positions, increase during periods of instability in exchange rates.

Interest rate risk refers to the exposure of a bank's financial condition to adverse moments in interest rates. The risk impacts both the earnings of a bank and the economic value of its assets, liabilities and off-balance sheet instruments. The primary forms of interest rate risk to which banks are typically exposed are: repricing risk, which arise from timing differences in the maturity (for fixed rate) and repricing (for floating rate) of banks' assets, liabilities and off-balance sheet positions; yield curve risk, which arises from changes in the slope and shape of the yield curve; basic risk, which arises from imperfect correlation in the adjustment of the rate earned and paid on different instruments with otherwise similar repricing characteristics, which arises from the express or implied options imbedded in many banks' assets, liabilities and off balance sheet portfolios.

Although it is a normal part of banking, excessive interest rate risk can be pose a significant threat to a bank's earnings and capital base. Managing this type of risk is of growing importance in sophisticated financial markets (with large interest rate exposures). Special attention should be paid to this risk in countries where interest rates are being deregulated.

1. In what ways do banks act as "market makers" in foreign exchange markets?

   A. by buying foreign currencies

   B. by quoting exchange rates to customers

   C. by avoiding the risks of the market

   D. Both A and B

2. Running open foreign exchange positions is_____, especially during periods of instability in exchange rates.

   A. of low risk   B. of high risk   C. of no risk   D. visible

3. How many forms of interest rate risk were mentioned in the passage?

   A. Five   B. Three   C. Two   D. Four

4. Repricing risk comes from_____.

   A. changes in the slope and shape of the yield curve

   B. the express or implied options imbedded in many banks' assets, liabilities and off-balance sheet portfolios

   C. timing differences in the maturity and repricing of banks' assets, liabilities and off-balance sheet positions

   D. None of the above

5. Excessive interest rate risk impacts_____.

   A. the earnings of a bank

   B. economic value of a bank's assets

   C. capital base of a bank

   D. All of the above

Chapter 3
Capital Markets

3.1　Purpose and Participants

Firms that issue capital market securities and the investors who buy them have very different motivations than they have when they operate in the money market. Firms and individuals use the money market primarily to warehouse funds for short periods of time until a more important need or a more productive use for the funds arises. By contrast, firms and individuals use the capital market for long-term investments. The capital markets provide an alternative to investment in assets such as real estate or gold. Meanwhile, the primary reason that individuals and firms choose to borrow long-term funds is to reduce the risk that interest rates will rise before they pay off their debt. This reduction in risk comes at a cost. However, Most long-term interest rates are higher than short-term rates due to risk premiums. Despite the need to pay higher interest rates to borrow in the capital markets, these markets remain very active.

The primary issuers of capital market securities are governments and corporations. However, governments never issue stocks.

Corporations both issue bonds and stocks. One of the most difficult decisions a firm faces can be whether it should finance its growth with debt or equity. The distribution of a firm's capital between debt and equity is its capital structure.

3.2　Trading in the Capital Market

Capital market trading occurs in either the primary market or the secondary market. Investment funds, corporations, and individual investors can all purchase securities offered in the primary market, where new issues of stocks and bonds are introduced. When firms sell securities for the first time, the issue is an initial public offering (IPO).

The capital markets have well-developed secondary market. A secondary market is where the sale of previously issued securities takes place, and it is important because most investors plan to sell long-term bonds before they reach maturity and eventually to sell their holdings of stocks as well.

1. Bonds

The capital markets are where securities with original maturities of greater than one year trade. Capital market securities fall into three categories: bonds, stocks, and mortgages. In this section, we focus on bonds.

Bonds are securities that represent a debt owed by the issuer to the investor. Bonds obligate the issuer to pay a specified amount at a given date.

Treasury Bonds

The government issues notes and bonds to finance the national debt. The difference between notes and bonds is that notes have a original maturity of 1 to 10 years while bonds have a original maturity of 10 to 30 years. (Recall from last chapter that Treasury bills mature in less than 1 year.)

Government notes and bonds are free of default risk because the government can always print money to pay off debt if necessary.

Corporate Bonds

When large corporations need to borrow funds for long periods of time, they may issue bonds. The bond indenture is a contract that states the lender's

Chapter 3   Capital Markets

rights and privileges and the borrower's obligations. Any collateral offered as security to the bondholders will also be described in the indenture.

The degree of risk varies widely among issues because the risk of default depends on the company's health, which can be affected by a number of variables. The interest rate on corporate bonds varies with the level of risk. Bonds issued by a company with high credit rating has lower interest rates than those with poor ratings.

2. Stocks

Shares of stock in the firm represent ownership. A stockholder owns a percentage interest in a firm consistent with the percentage of outstanding stock held. The ownership is in contrast to a bondholder, who holds no ownership interest but is rather a creditor of the firm.

Investors can earn a return from stocks in one of two years. Either the price of the stock rises over time, or the firm pays the stockholder dividends. Frequently, investors earn a return from both sources. Stocks are more risky than bonds because stockholders have a lower priority than bondholders when the firm is in trouble. The returns to investors are less assured because dividends can be easily changed, and stock price increases are not guaranteed. Despite these risks, it is possible to make a great deal of money by investing in stocks, whereas it is very unlikely by investing in bonds. Another distinction between stocks and bonds is that stocks do not mature.

Ownership of stocks gives the stockholder certain rights regarding the firm. One is the right of a residual claimant: Stockholders have a claim on all assets and income left over after all other claimants have been satisfied. If nothing is left over, they get nothing. As noted, however, it is possible to get rich as a stockholder if the firm does well.

参考译文

第3章 资本市场

3.1 资本市场的目的和参与者

在资本市场上，企业发行证券和投资者购买证券与他们在货币市场上的运作有着截然不同的动机。企业和个人利用货币市场来存放短期资金直到有更重要或更有效使用资金的途径出现。相比之下，企业和个人利用资本市场主要是为了长期投资。资本市场为其他资产(如实物资产和黄金资产)的投资提供了一个替代性的投资方法。与此同时，个人和企业选择借入长期资金的首要原因是为了降低在他们偿还债务之前利率上升的风险。但这一风险的减少是有代价的。因为，由于风险溢价大多数长期利率高于短期利率。尽管资本市场需要支付较高的利率借入资金，这些市场仍然非常活跃。

资本市场证券的主要发行者是政府和企业。不过，政府从来不发行股票。

企业既可以发行债券，也可以发行股票。企业面临的最困难的决定之一是以债权还是股权来进行融资。企业资本中债务资本和股权资本的分配是公司的资本结构问题。

3.2 资本市场的交易

资本市场的交易既可发生在初级市场，也可发生在二级市场。投资基金、公司和个人投资者都能在初级市场上购买新发行的股票和债券。当公司第一次出售该公司证券，即为首次公开发行(IPO)。

资本市场有相当发达的二级市场。二级市场是已发行的证券进行再出售的市场，这一点极为重要，因为大多数投资者计划在到期之前出售长期债券，并且最终出售他们所持有的股票。

1. 债券

资本市场是到期日超过一年以上的证券交易的市场。资本市场的证券分为三种类型：债券、股票和抵押。本节重点介绍债券。

债券是代表债券发行人所欠投资者债务的凭证。债券发行人有义务在约定日期支付规定的金额给债券持有者。

国债

政府发行中期和长期债券为国家债务融资。中期债券和长期债券的区别是中期债券的期限为1～10年，而长期债券的期限为10～30年。(在第1章中曾介绍国库券的期限不超过1年。)

政府债券没有违约风险，因为政府可以在必要的时候印制钞票来偿还债务。

公司债券

当大公司需要借入长期资金时，也可以发行债券。债券合约规定了贷款人的权利和特权以及借款人的义务。任何提供给持票人的抵押担保也必须记载在契约中。

不同公司的债券风险程度差别很大，因为违约的风险取决于该公司的经营状况，这受很多因素的影响。公司债券的利息取决于其风险程度。信用评级高的公司发行的债券利率要低于那些信用评级低的公司。

2. 股票

股票代表了公司的所有权。股东拥有的股息的比例与其持有的公司流通股比例相一致。所有权与债券持有人不同，债券持有人只是公司的债权人，并不拥有公司的所有权带来的股息。

投资者可以在一两年内赚取股票的利润。不管是股价在这段时间内上升，还是公司给股东支付股息。通常情况下，投资者同时通过这两个途径赚取利润。股票的风险比债券更大，因为在公司遇到困难时，股东的优先清偿权比债券持有人低。股票给投资者的回报不太确定，因为股息很容易变化，股票价格的上升也无法得到保证。尽管有这些风险，通过投资股票投资者还是有可能赚大钱，但如果投资债券则不太可能。股票和债券的另一个区别是股票没有到期日。

股票的所有权赋予股东关于公司的一些权利。其中之一是剩余索取权：在其他债权人都得到清偿后，如果还有剩余，股东有权获得剩余财产。但如果没有任何剩余财产，股东就会一无所获。不过，如前所述，如果公司经营状态良好，股东就有可能富裕起来。

Chapter 3 Capital Markets

Subject Topic(命题对话)

The Future Financial Centers of China

(中国未来的金融中心)

A: As we all know, both Hong Kong and Shanghai are going to be China's future financial centers. But I think they have their respective characteristics. Do you think so?

B: Yes. Hong Kong is a free port and one of the world's most important markets for gold, foreign exchange and capital everyday. Capital from all over the world flows in and out freely. It has a highly advanced communication network. At the same time, It possesses a management advantage with advanced service industries and numerous qualified personnel. It also has a favorable market environment. However, Hong Kong has its difficulties, such as narrow space, high service cost and more challenges from new financial centers such as Singapore and Taiwan. However, as a financial center with a free capitalist system, Hong Kong would forever be a joint point of Sino-European civilization. It is a bridge that links China with the rest of the world.

A: That is true. Compared with Hong Kong, Shanghai also enjoys a great deal of advantages, like wider space and lower service cost. The production capacity of Shanghai is immense. If Shanghai fully exerts its production capacity, it would become incomparable in the future. Since Shanghai has a large population and is the economic center of the Yangtze Valley, its market is extensive. Moreover, in recent years, its investment environment has become more and more favorable. Therefore, a large number of multinational companies and foreign-funded institutions have been attracted to establish

39

their branches there. There foreign investments have stimulated the economic development of Shanghai. In addition, Pudong has opened up and become the financial core of Shanghai.

B: What you have said is right, but I think if Shanghai wants to become one of the top financial centers in Asia, it should further improve itself. First of all, it should maintain a sound socialist market-oriented economy with a complete legal system in the financial field as the basis. Secondly, it should form a highly advanced financial market system. The system should include an open market for foreign exchange, gold and capital. Next, it should attract more qualified personnel. They should be equipped with comprehensive knowledge in management, finance, trade and foreign languages. Its service industry and infrastructure construction should also be improved. Finally, Shanghai should fully exert its potential to become a highly developed financial center.

A: I quite agree with you. Nowadays, with the opening up of China's financial field, foreign-funded banks and domestic banks will become intense. Is this beneficial to China's financial industry?

B: Yes, the intense competition could in some way benefit China's financial development. It will stimulate domestic banks to improve their management, operation and services. At the same time, foreign-funded banks in China will bring us advanced knowledge, experience and practice in management. Moreover, the intense competition will help to create a favorable investment environment in China. More opportunities would be provided for domestic banks to engage in international operations. Finally, it will promote fair competition in China's economic field as well. However, the intense competition will also influence China's financial environment. For one thing, compared with domestic banks, foreign-funded banks possess advantages in management, technology, service and qualified personnel. The competition

Chapter 3　Capital Markets

will inevitably make domestic banks lose part of their traditional business to foreign-funded banks. The competition will also probably bring difficulties to the central bank's financial supervision. Since foreign-funded banks' operation observes international practice, it differs from that of domestic banks. Therefore, it challenges the efficiency of the central bank's supervision.

Questions and Answers(专业问答)

1.　What are the intermediate objectives of monetary policies?

　—a. Growth in money supply;

　　b. Interest rate level;

　　c. Growth in the volume of credit;

　　d. The exchange rate.

2.　Please point out the full name of SWIFT and its headquarter.

　— Society for World Inter-bank Financial Telecommunications. Brussels, Belgian.

3.　What is the biggest difference between off-balance sheet activities and intermediary activities of commercial banks?

　—Off-balance sheet activities constitute potential assets or liabilities and bear certain risk while intermediary activities don't constitute risks in assets or liabilities.

4.　What is the main body of offshore financial market?

　— It is non-residents.

41

Exercises(练习)

Reading Comprehension

Passage One

Apart from borrowing from banks, a firm or an individual can obtain funds in a financial market in two ways. The most common method is to issue a debt instrument, such as a bond or a mortgage, which is a contractual agreement by the borrower to pay the holder of the instrument fixed amounts at regular intervals(interest and principal payment) until a specified date(the maturity date), when a final payment is made. The maturity of debt instrument is the time(term) to the instrument's expiration date. A debt instrument is short-term if its maturity is less than a year and long-term if its maturity is ten years or longer. Debt instruments with a maturity between one and ten years are said to be intermediate-term.

The second method of raising funds is by issuing equities, such as common stock, which are claim to share in the net income(income after expenses and taxes) and the assets of a business. If you own one share of common stock in a company that has issued one million shares, you are entitled to one millionth of the firm's net income and one millionth of the firm's assets. Equities usually earn periodic payments(dividends) and are considered long-term securities because they have no maturity date.

The main disadvantage of owning a corporation's equities rather than its debt is that an equity holder is a residual claimant; that is, the corporation must pay all its mature debt holders before it pays its equity holders. The advantage of holding equities is that equity holders benefit directly from any increase in the corporation's profitability or asset value because equities confer ownership rights on the equity holders. Debt holders do not share in this benefit because

Chapter 3   Capital Markets

their dollar payments are fixed.

1. A firm or an individual can raise funds_____.

A. by borrowing from banks

B. by issuing a debt instrument

C. by issuing equities

D. All of the above

2. A bond is long-term if its maturity is_____.

A. between one and ten years

B. is less than a year

C. ten years or longer

D. within 20 years

3. Common stock refers to____.

A. claims to share in the net income of a business

B. preferred stock

C. claims to share in the net income and the assets of a business

D. claims to dividends

4. That "equity holder" is "a residual claims" means_____.

A. the corporation must pay its equity holder only after paying its mature debt holders

B. the equity holder enjoys the privilege of being paid first

C. the equity holder will be neglected

D. the equity older will be looked down upon

5. Holding a firm's equities is advantageous than owning its debts in that_____.

A. debt holders share the benefit of any profit increase of the firm

B. equity holders benefit directly from any increase of the profitability or asset value of the firm

C. equities give ownership rights to the equity holders

D. Both B and C

43

Passage Two

A primary market is a financial market in which new issues of a security, such as a bond or a stock, are sold to initial buyers by the corporation or government agency borrowing the funds. A secondary market is a financial market in which securities that have been previously issued(and are thus secondhand) can be sold.

The primary markets for securities are not well known to the public because the selling of securities to initial buyers takes place behind closed doors. An important financial institution that assists in the initial sale of securities in the primary market is the investment bank. It does this by underwriting securities, that is, it guarantees a price for a corporation's securities and then sell them to the public.

The New York Stock Exchange (NYSE), in which previously issued stocks are traded, is the best-known example of secondary markets, although the bond markets, in which previously issued bonds of major corporations and the US government are bought and sold, actually have a larger trading volume. Other examples of secondary markets are foreign exchange markets, futures markets, and options markets. Securities brokers and dealers are crucial to a well-functioning secondary market. Brokers are agents of investors who match buyers with sellers of securities; dealers link buyers and sellers by buying and selling securities at stated prices.

1.   A primary market is_____.

A. a financial market where new issues of a security are resold public
   to initial buyers

B. a financial market where previously traded securities are sold to
   initial buyers

C. a financial market where new securities are sold to initial buyers
   behind closed doors

D. a financial market in which securities are resold to initial buyers

Chapter 3　Capital Markets

behind closed doors

2. A secondary market is_____.

A. informal and illegal

B. a financial market in which previously traded securities or stocks are normally resold through an investment bank

C. a financial market where previously issued stocks are resold behind the closed doors

D. a financial market in which secondhand securities are resold

3. Underwriting securities means_____.

A. fixing the prices of buying and selling only

B. buying securities and selling them to public

C. being responsible for writing the documents concerning securities

D. All of the above

4. Brokers are_____.

A. financial intermediaries

B. agents of investors who bring together the sellers and buyers of securities

C. agent that provide information that the buyers and sellers need to strike a bargain

D. All of the above

5. Dealers_____.

A. have the same functions as brokers

B. link buyers and sellers

C. buy and sell securities at stated prices

D. Both B and C

Passage Three

Merger and acquisitions simply mean that one company would attempt to take over another by gaining enough of its common stock to gain control. In the simplest sense, merger refers to that two companies become one with the

45

acquirer being in the commanding position.

Merger comes in one of several distinct forms. A horizontal merger brings together two companies in a similar industry, two steel companies for example. A vertical merger brings together two companies in related industries. A steel company taking over an energy producer such as a coal mine would be an example. An automobile producer taking over a parts manufacturer is another. In either case, the merger is designed to produce a synergy between the two companies that did not exist before. The horizontal merger should produce greater scale and efficiency, avoiding duplication of products and production. Both bring together companies related either directly or indirectly.

Another type of merger, or takeover as the case may be, is the merger of two unrelated companies. This is known as the conglomerate merger means a company purposely buying another not engaged in the same business at all. This sort of merger and the conglomerates it creates were originally conceived to serve as hedge against changing economic climates.

Leveraged buyout (LBO) is the purchase of one company by another using mainly borrowed funds.

Generally most M&A activity involves one company buying another, taking it out of the public marketplace. On occasion, the management of a company will itself tender for the outstanding shares of a company, accomplishing the same ends. This type of privatization is referred to as a management buyout, or MBO.

Acquisitions are classified as either friendly or hostile, depending upon the reaction of the target company's directly to the proposed bid. If management remains opposed and attempts to dissuade shareholders from accepting the offer of the acquirer, the proposed purchase price is known as a hostile offer, as opposed to a friendly offer if they agree to the terms and conditions. But it should not be assumed that all hostile bids will be successful. Target companies can mount expensive defense to ward off unwanted suitors, although the costs

Chapter 3　Capital Markets

can be quite high. Some of those defenses are also products of the 1980s and are equally or more famous than some of the financial engineering techniques developed during the same period.

1. Merger and acquisitions means _____.

   A. two companies becoming one with the acquirer being in a subordinate position

   B. one company taking over by acquiring enough of its common stock

   C. two companies forming a synergy that did not exit before

   D. Both B and C

2. What is a conglomerate?

   A. It is a merger of two related industries.

   B. It is a company deliberately acquiring another engaged in an activity different from that of the original.

   C. It is a vertical merger.

   D. It is a hostile merger.

3. Leveraged buyout refers to _____.

   A. the acquisition of one company by another through its influence

   B. the buying of one company by another mainly using debt

   C. the acquiring of one company by force

   D. the buying of one company by diversifying the risks

4. MBO refer to_____.

   A. the management of a company voluntarily offering to buy the outstanding shares of a company

   B. a company buying another, taking it out of the public marketplace

   C. management buyout

   D. Both A and C

5. What does a hostile acquisition mean?

   A. It means the target companies disagree to the terms and conditions proposed by the acquirer.

47

B. It means the management of the target companies opposes the proposed bid but tries to persuade shareholders to accept the offer of the acquirer.

C. All hostile bids fail.

D. Target companies may try to keep away from unwanted suitors, usually at modest costs.

Chapter 4
Foreign Exchange Markets

4.1　Meanings of Foreign Exchange

The term "foreign exchange" has three principal meanings. In the first place, it means the system utilized in financing international payments. Or it may refer to the subject which is studied to obtain knowledge as to the financial operations conducted to discharge international obligations.

In the second place, it means the media used to discharge international obligations. For the purpose of international finance and exchange, the principal kinds of media are telegraphic transfers, mail transfers, bills, demand drafts, cheques, banker's drafts, foreign bonds, coupons, dividend checks, pension checks, commercial and personal letters of credit, traveller's cheques, foreign notes and coins, etc..

The third meaning of the term "foreign exchange" is that it covers, in a general way, the rates at which foreign exchange is quoted.

The overwhelming majority of international payments are made through the media of foreign exchange traded in foreign exchange markets. The foreign exchange market is not an organized market in the same sense as a stock exchange or commodity exchange. In other words, there is no single, physical place where purchases and sales are executed. While markets are organized in various ways in different countries of the world, most foreign exchange transactions are simply arranged by two parties and executed by telephone or telex. The most important dealers which maintain foreign exchange "dealing rooms" and execute foreign exchange transactions between themselves's markets perform four major functions: (1) transfer of payments, (2) the provision of credit, (3) payment at a distance, and (4) allowing hedging against exchange risks.

The method of quoting the prices or rates of exchange for different currencies takes one of two forms, the direct quotation method and the indirect quotation method. Under the direct quotation method, the rates are quoted in terms of a variable number of home currency per fixed foreign currency unit, and China adopts this method. Under the indirect quotation method, the units to the fixed unit of home currency, the exchange market in London practices this method.

An exchange dealer always quotes two rates, at one of which he will buy and at the other of which he will sell the foreign currency. For direct rates then, on the standpoint of the exchange dealer, the maxim is "buy low, sell high", for indirect rates, the maxim is "buy high, sell low".

A distinction must be drawn between rates quoted by a dealer to his customers and the so-called "market rates". The market rates are those ruling between the dealers themselves as members of the market. For direct rates, the selling rate to his customers will be higher than that of the market rate, while the buying rate will be lower than that of the market rate. There are many other exchange expressions, but those who are not well versed in exchange terminology would do well to confine themselves to the use of the expressions "favourable" and "unfavourable" when describing movements in exchange from the point of view of their countries, or to the use of "appreciate" and "depreciate" when describing a movement in the value of any particular currency. In the case of direct rates, "low rates are for us" (favourable from a national viewpoint) and "high rates are against us" (unfavourable from a national viewpoint) ; or vice versa in the case of indirect rates.

All claims to foreign currency payable abroad, whether consisting of funds

Chapter 4 Foreign Exchange Markets

held (in foreign currency) with banks abroad, or bills or cheques, again in foreign currency and payable abroad, are termed foreign exchange. All these claims play a part in the relations between a bank and its customers. In the trading of foreign exchange between banks, which is the job of the foreign exchange dealer, only foreign currency held with banks abroad is concerned. For the purposes of this book, the term "foreign exchange" applies only to bank balances denominated in foreign currency.

Foreign bank notes are not foreign exchange in the narrower sense. They can be converted into foreign exchange, however, provided they can be placed without restriction to the credit of an ordinary commercial account abroad. The exchange regulations of some countries do not allow this conversion of bank notes into foreign exchange, although the operation in reverse is nearly always permitted.

A currency, whether in foreign exchange or bank notes, is usually called convertible if the person holding it can convert it, in other words change it, freely into another currency. A distinction needs to be made, however, between unrestricted convertibility and the various forms of partial convertibility. The Swiss franc, for example, is fully convertible whether the holder is resident in Switzerland or abroad, and regardless of whether current payments or financial transactions are concerned.

The banks are the natural intermediary between foreign supply and demand. The main task of a bank's foreign exchange department is to enable its commercial or financial customers to convert assets held in one currency into funds of another currency. This conversion can take the form of a "spot" transaction or a "forward" operation. Banking activities in the foreign exchange field tend inevitably to establish a uniform price range for a particular currency throughout the financial centers of the world. If at a given moment the market rate in one center deviates too far from the average, a balance will soon be restored by arbitrage, which is the process of taking advantage of price differences in different places. It can be seen that the foreign exchange market acts as a very important regulator in a free monetary system.

Only the big banks and a number of local banks specializing in this kind of business have a foreign exchange department with qualified dealers. Banks which merely carry out their customers' instructions and do no business on their own account do not really require the services of a foreign exchange expert. For these it will be sufficient to have someone with a general knowledge of the subject because his role in practice will be that of an intermediary between the customer and a bank professionally in the market.

A foreign exchange dealer acquires his professional skill largely through experience. Here we should point out how important close cooperation is among a team of dealers. The group can work together smoothly only if each member is able to shed his individuality. We must not forget that, almost incessantly, all the dealers are doing business simultaneously on different telephones, and when large transactions are completed the rates may change, whereupon the other dealers must be brought up to date immediately. It is essential for a dealer to have the knack of doing two things at once so that he can do business on the telephone and at the same time take note of the new prices announced by his colleagues.

Professional foreign exchange dealing requires advanced technical equipment. Business is done by telephone (with many direct lines to important names) and teleprinter, depending on distance and convenience. At many modern banks, the foreign exchange department uses the Reuters dealing system, which combines the functions of a teleprinter with those of a television screen. Spot and forward rates of the most important currencies and money market rates are displayed on a number of rate boards, remote-controlled by the chief dealers. Current quotations can then not only be used by the bank's own dealers but also transmitted electronically to other banks. Electronic data-processing equipment is employed to keep track instantly of the exchange positions, and for the

Chapter 4   Foreign Exchange Markets

administrative handling of the business done. Cross rates are worked out with the help of electronic desk-top calculators.

4.2   Financial Derivatives

4.2.1   Spot Transaction

Spot transaction means the actual and variable amount of the currency of one country which at any given time, can be bought for a fixed sum in the currency of another country. It is a term meaning that these transactions are settled the second working day from the date of the deal.

Example: On Oct. 10th I buy/sell value Oct. 12th.

The "value date" given to a transaction is the date on which the money must be paid to the parties involved. For all spot, or current, exchange operations the value date is set as the second working day after the date on which the transaction is concluded (to allow for the administrative handling of the deals). Since banks are closed in the western world on Saturdays and Sundays, spot deals made on Thursday will show Monday as value or settlement date.

It is possible, though exceptional, to conclude foreign exchange transactions for delivery one business day after conclusion of the deal (or sometimes even value same day). Such deals will however not be made at the quoted spot rates but a slightly different rates, depending on the interest rates for the currencies concerned.

4.2.2   Forward Operations

Foreign exchange can be bought and sold not only on a spot or cash basis, but also on a forward basis (for delivery on a stipulated future date). Theoretically, the forward price for a currency can be identical with the spot price. Almost always, however, the forward price in practice is either higher (premium) or lower (discount) than the spot price.

Forward transactions can serve a number of different purposes. First of all, by doing forward transactions one can cover, or hedge an otherwise existing exchange risk, which is of a commercial (trade) or financial nature. In connection with money market (deposit) transactions, we encounter the swap operation, which is the combination of a spot purchase with a simultaneous forward sale (or vice versa). To avoid confusion when talking about forward business, dealers use the term "outright" operation when it is a single forward transaction, as against a forward transaction forming part of a swap operation. Outright deals can, as just seen, be a hedge; however, they are speculative transactions if they lack a commercial or financial background.

International trade always creates the need for forward operations, if the exchange risk is to be hedged. Let us consider the case of a Swiss importer who has bought goods in UK, invoiced in Sterling Pounds, payable in 90 days. To eliminate the risk of a significant rise of the Sterling Pounds in the meantime — and also to have the basis for an exact price calculation — he buys the Sterling Pounds 90 days forward (outright). In the converse case a Swiss exporter knows that in three months he will receive Euro in payment for his exports. Here again, in order to eliminate the exchange risk, he hedges by selling the Euros three months forward (outright). Not to do these forward transactions would be equivalent to speculating, on a fall of the Sterling Pounds in the first case, or a rise of the Euros in the second case.

Currency exposures, and thus the need to hedge them, can also arise from a variety of non-trade operations:

- Securities investments, money market deposits, loans extended to subsidiaries abroad, direct investments, etc., if done in foreign currencies all represent foreign currency assets; the currency risk can be covered by selling the respective currency forward.

Chapter 4   Foreign Exchange Markets

- Borrowings in capital markets abroad, for instance, if done in foreign currencies, represent foreign currency liabilities; the inherent exchange risk can be hedged by forward purchases of the respective currency.

In this connection, it should be noted that hedging by means of forward operations is possible even if the underlying transaction is of a medium — or long-term nature. For many currencies, forward deals of more than twelve months are difficult to arrange, but by regularly renewing, say, a twelve-month forward contract at maturity, we can match the hedge with the tenor of the underlying longer-term transaction. True, in such a case one only knows the cost of the hedging for the first period while the costs for the ensuing periods are not known in advance; this, however, need not be a reason for not hedging.

It should be pointed out here that, contrary to widespread belief, hedging does not necessarily involve costs. One normally hedges "weak" currencies against "stronger" ones, by selling the former forward, and to many people "weak" currencies are those with a discount; in such cases hedging involve costs. Yet, it has happened many times that the supposedly "weak" currency strengthened, while the supposedly "strong" one (with a premium) declined. Examples: From February to October 1992, sterling weakened from $1.82 to $1.61, although the pound was always at a premium. From the end of 1982 to the beginning of 1985, the dollar strengthened against most other hard currencies despite the fact that it was constantly at a discount. In these special instances, it would have been advisable to hedge sterling and German marks against dollars (i.e. buy forward dollars). This would not only have prevented an exchange loss but even yielded a hedging "profit"!

4.2.3 Swaps

It contains two simultaneous inseparable contract-deals, the first for spot delivery, and the second (the contrary of spot) for future delivery (in this case

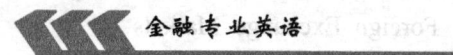

your position is squared).

Or, in other words: the simultaneous purchase and sale of identical amounts of a currency for different value dates.

Swaps can be done for fixed periods:

- "overnight swap"
- "tomorrow / next swap"
- "spot / next swap"
- "week / end swap"
- "1, 2, 3, etc. months swap" or for broken periods: 45, 65, 95 days.

4.2.4 Futures

Futures are forward transactions which are traded on exchanges, i.e. not OTC (over-the-counter). In order to be marketable on exchanges, futures are standardized in terms of quantity, settlement dates and quotation. While, currency futures have not been able to get established in Europe due to the efficient and more flexible forward exchange business, interest rate futures have achieved some significance. A lot has been heard about financial innovations over the last few years in general, and in particular, standardized futures. In this context, numerous new products have been developed on American forward exchanges. Together with the traditional forward transactions in goods and metals (commodity futures), a large number of financial forward contracts (financial futures) exist today on various exchanges. These include futures on stocks, interest rates, currencies and stock indexes. Since November 9, 1990, contracts on stock-index futures with the Swiss Market Index (SMI) as a reference have been traded on the SOFFEX (Swiss Options and Financial Futures Exchange). Within the Swiss Bank Corporation Group, interest rate and currency options are traded via SBCI Futures Inc., New York.

4.2.5 Currency and Interest Rate Options

With the transition to floating exchange rates, central banks were no longer obliged to maintain exchange rates within narrow limits as defined in the Bretton Woods Agreement. Continuing disequilibria in international balances of payments led to increasing fluctuations in exchange rates especially after the liberalization of cross-border capital movements. The need to eliminate currency risks therefore became extremely urgent. The market for foreign exchange options, set up in the early 1980's, was a decisive step in minimizing exchange rate risks and creating greater flexibility than had previously been possible with existing instruments.

Whereas a forward transaction provides the possibility of setting an exchange rate for a future foreign exchange transaction, the buyer of the option acquires the right, but not the obligation, to go ahead with the contract, i.e. to take up the option or to allow it to expire. It is therefore possible to hedge against a currency loss as well as to benefit from any profit on a foreign exchange transaction.

The following are types of (European) option contracts.

1. Call Option

The right to buy a certain amount of a currency at a fixed rate (strike price) at a pre-arranged expiry date.

2. Put Option

The right to sell a certain amount of a currency at a fixed rate (strike price) at a pre-arranged expiry date.

It should be noted that the right does not imply the obligation to exercise an option.

The buyer of an option decides whether or not he will take up (call) or supply (put) the amount of a currency stipulated in the contract and pays a premium for this right. The seller (option writer) has no choice in either case and for this he receives the premium from the buyer which has to be paid to close the contract.

4.3　Exchange Control

Exchange control means official control in the foreign exchange dealings of a country. The control may extend over a wide area, covering the import and export of goods and services, remittances from the country, inflow and outflow of capital, rate of exchange, method of payment, maintenance of balance in foreign centers, acquisition and holding of foreign securities, financial relationship between residents and non-residents. Exchange control restricts the right of holders of a currency to exchange it for other currencies. It thereby renders a currency inconvertible.

The main objects of exchange control resorted by most developing countries are to prevent pressures on balance of payments from adversely affecting official holding of international reserves or the local currency's external value, to bring the balance of payments into equilibrium and insure that the flow of trade and capital contributes to their development goals.

Besides the control on the import and export of goods, the other methods used for exchange control are: (1) control of the ports and exports should be made and received, to and from specified countries, and (2) bilateral agreements between two countries contracted principally for the purpose of avoiding the balance of payments deficit.

The responsibility for enforcing exchange control laws, regulations and coordinating exchange control policy generally rests with the ministry of finance. The administering of the exchange control regulations is often entrusted to a

Chapter 4 Foreign Exchange Markets

central bank, but there are many cases where this task is divided among a number of departments or agencies, each with control over specific international transactions. In China, the People's Bank of China exercises the foreign exchange control laws and regulations. The day-to-day operation of exchange control is often conducted to handle all foreign currency transactions in accordance with the government's exchange control regulations. It is usually the bank's duty to insure that receipts and payments of foreign currency are generated by valid legal transactions.

Exchange control system varies from country to country. Most countries adopt single-rate systems in which all foreign exchange transactions are carried on at one official rate of exchange. Single-rate systems are administered by an exchange control authority that is the sole buyer and seller of foreign exchange. Exporters and others who receive foreign exchange from foreign residents are to surrender it to the control authority at the official rate. Importers and others who want to make payments to foreign residents must obtain permission to buy foreign exchange from the control authority at the official rate. The control authority may also regulates the use of domestic currency (bank account) owned by foreign residents. Commercial banks are usually authorized to act as buying and selling agents of the exchange control authority. Single exchange-rate systems are usually strengthened by a system of import quota and / or import licences, and export licences. Ordinarily the import licence also serves as an exchange licence. In some countries, however, an exchange licence is needed in addition to an import licence.

参考译文

第4章 外 汇 市 场

4.1 外汇的含义

"外汇"这一术语有三个主要含义。 首先，它是指国际支付融资中所使用的系统。或者它可以被认为是一门研究清偿国际债权债务中金融运作的学科。

其次，外汇是指用来清偿履行国际债权债务的支付手段。进行国际融资和汇兑主要支付手段有：电汇，信汇，票据，即期汇票，支票，银行汇票，外国债券，息票，股利支票，年金支票、商业和个人信用证，旅行支票，外国纸币和硬币等。

"外汇"的第三个含义是指汇率，即不同外汇的交换比率。

绝大多数国际支付是通过外汇市场上的外汇交易进行的。外汇市场和证券交易所或商品交易不一样，它并不是一个有组织的市场。换句话说，它没有一个买卖外汇的有形交易场所。虽然世界上不同国家的交易双方可以通过不同的方式进行外汇买卖，大多数外汇交易还是通过电话或电传进行的。一些重要的外汇交易商之间进行外汇交易以保持外汇市场的流动性，他们的作用主要有四个。

(1) 转付款项。

(2) 提供信用。

(3) 远距离付款。

(4) 对冲汇兑风险。

不同货币之间的标价或兑换比率的标示采用以下两种不同的方式之一：直接标价法和间接标价法。在直接标价法下，以固定的外国货币为标准来计算应付出多少单位本国货币，中国采取这个方法。在间接标价法下，以固定单位的本国货币为标准，来计算应收若干单位的外国货币，伦敦外汇市场就使用这种方法。

外汇交易商总会标出两个外汇汇率，一个是他买入外汇的价格，一个是他卖出外汇的价格。在直接标价法下，外汇交易商是"低买高卖"。在间接标价法下，外汇交易商是"高买低卖"。

这里必须要指出外汇交易商对其客户的汇率标价和市场汇率的区别。市场汇率是那些外汇交易商之间作为外汇市场的成员进行交易的市价。在直接标价法下，外汇交易商给客户的卖价会高于市场汇率，而买价会低于市场汇率。还有其他许多外汇术语，但是对于那些不精通外汇术语的人，最好还是用"顺差"和"逆差"来描述外汇在国家之间的流动，或者用"升值"或"贬值"来描述某一种货币价值的变动。在直接标价法下，低汇率是对我们是有利的(从国家的角度)，高汇率对我们是不利的(从国家的角度)。在间接标价法下刚好相反。

以外币形式支付的所有债权，不管是存放在海外银行的外币资金还是支付给国外的以外币计价的票据或支票，都称为外汇。所有这些债权在银行和它的顾客之间起着作用。由外汇交易员进行的银行之间的外汇交易，只有海外银行持有的外币才被认为是外汇。本书中"外汇"一词仅指银行的外币存款余额。

外国钞票不是狭义的外汇。然而它们可以兑换成外汇，假如它们可以不受限制地存放在国外的一个普通的商业往来账户上。某些国家的外汇管理条例不允许把外国钞票兑换成外汇，虽然几乎都允许把外汇兑换成外币。

只要货币的持有人能兑换某种货币，不管是以外汇形式还是以外国钞票的形式，则这一货币为可兑换的，换句话说，它可以自由地兑换成其他货币。这里需要区分无限制的可兑换和各种形式的部分可兑换。例如，瑞士法郎是完全可兑换的，不管持有人是瑞士居民还是非居民，不管是经常性支出还是金融交易。

银行是外汇供给和需求的中介。银行外汇部门的主要任务是帮助它的顾客把一种货币的资产转换成另一种货币。这一兑换可以采取"即期"交易或"远期"交易的形式。在外汇市场上，通过国际金融中心，银行的业务活动会使某一货币形成一致的价格范围。如果在某一时刻，某一国际金融中心的汇率远远偏离了其平均价，市场上的套汇行为会使市场马上恢复平衡。套汇是利用不同市场的汇率价格差异进行低买高卖获取利润。由此可见，外汇市场可以被看作自由货币制度下的一个非常重要的管理者。

只有大银行和一些本地银行专门从事外汇业务，他们的外汇交易部门有合格的外汇交易员。那些仅仅履行客户的指令进行外汇交易，并没有以自己的账户进行交易的银行并不真正需要外汇专家的服务。因此，有些银行只需要一些具备外汇基本知识的员工就足够了，实际上，他只是客户和银行之间的一个专业中介。

外汇交易员主要通过经验获得专业技能。这里我们应当指出外汇交易员团队紧密合作的重要性。只有当每名成员都发挥他的特长，整个团队才能顺利发展。所有外汇交易员不间断地，通过不同的电话同时进行交易。当大额交易完成时汇率可能会发生变化，在这种情况下，其他交易员必须立即提供最新的报价。外汇交易员必须有同时做两件事情的诀窍，这样他才能一边通过电话进行交易，同时注意他同事宣布的新价格。

专业的外汇交易要求有先进的技术设备。根据距离和方便性，交易通过电话(有许多联系重要客户的直通线路)和电传机完成。许多现代银行的外汇交易部门使用路透交易系统，它结合了电传机的功能和电视的显示功能。通过首席交易员的远程控制，主要货币的即期汇率和远期汇率以及货币市场的利率可以在屏幕上显示。银行当前的报价不仅可以被银行自己的交易员使用，还可以电子传送给其他银行。电子数据处理设备被用来随时追踪外汇头寸，以便管理业务的处理。汇率可以在桌上电子计算机的帮助下计算出。

4.2 金融衍生工具

4.2.1 即期外汇交易

即期外汇交易是指在任何特定时间，可以用一国货币购买另一国货币。即期外汇交易在交易日后的两个营业日内进行交割。

例：我在 10 月 10 日买入/卖出，交割日为 10 月 12 日。

外汇交易中约定的交割日是指货币必须支付给有关交易各方的日期。对所有的即期外汇交易，交割日为交易结束后的第二个工作日(以便于管理交易)。因为西方国家的银行在双休日停止营业，在周四交易的即期交易交割日或结算日为下周一。

外汇交易也有可能在交易日后的一个工作日就进行交割(有时甚至同一天交割)。但是这类交易采用的汇率与即期汇率标价略有不同，这取决于所交易货币的利率。

4.2.2　远期外汇交易

外汇交易不仅可以在即期进行买卖，也可以在远期进行买卖(即在约定的未来某一日期进行交割)。从理论上说，某种货币的远期汇率可以与即期汇率相同。但是绝大多数情况下，实际的远期汇率总是高于(远期升水)或低于(远期贴水)即期汇率。

远期外汇交易有很多作用。首先，可以通过远期外汇交易规避或对冲外汇风险，无论是商业(贸易)方面的还是财务方面的。与货币市场的(存款)交易相联系，我们可以进行掉期交易，即买入即期和卖出远期相结合(或相反)。为了避免混淆，当进行单一的远期外汇交易时，交易者使用术语"直接"远期外汇交易，以与掉期业务中的远期外汇交易区分开。直接远期外汇交易可以是套期保值，但如果缺乏商业或财务背景，直接远期外汇交易也可以是投机交易。

国际贸易常常需要远期外汇交易来对冲汇率风险。我们来看这样一个案例，瑞士进口商从英国购买了货物，以英镑计价，90 天内付款。为了减少英镑升值带来的风险，同时也为了有一个确切的计算价格的基础，他购买了 90 天的远期英镑。相反的例子，如果瑞士的出口商知道他出口的货物在三个月内会收到欧元款项。同样为了减少汇率风险，它可以出售三个月的远期欧元来对冲风险。如果不做这些远期外汇交易则等同于投机，如在第一个案例中如果英镑贬值则投机获利，而第二个案例中如果欧元升值则投机获利。

非贸易业务也会带来汇率风险，需要采取措施进行套期保值。

- 证券投资、货币市场存款、给国外的子公司的贷款和直接投资等，如果以外币计价都代表外币资产；由此带来的汇率风险可以通过出售相应货币的远期外汇来规避。

- 在国外资本市场的借款，如果以外币计价则代表外币债务，其固有的汇兑风险也可以通过购买相应货币的远期外汇来套期保值。

在这里需要指出，中长期交易的汇率风险也可以通过远期外汇交易来套期保值。虽然大部分货币没有超过 12 个月的远期交易，但是通过展期，也就是说，12 个月的远期合约到期时，我们可以通过签订新的与长期交易的时间匹配的远期交易合约来对冲风险。诚然，在这种情况下，客户只知道第一阶段的对冲费用，而随后阶段的对冲费用事先并不知道。但是，我们不能因为这个原因就不进行套期保值。

应该指出，与前述相反，套期保值并不一定要支付费用。一般人们会通过出售弱货币与强货币进行对冲，大多数人认为弱货币未来会贴水，在这种情况下，套期保值需要成本。然而，在很多情况下预计贴水的弱货币会升值，而预计升水的强货币会贬值。例如，从 1992 年 2 月—10 月英镑从 1.82 美元/英镑跌至 1.61 美元/英镑，虽然远期英镑总是升水。从 1982 年底至 1985 年初，美元对大多数其他硬货币走强，尽管远期美元时常贴水。在这种特殊情况下，用英镑和德国马克对美元进行套期保值是可取的(即购买远期美元)。这不仅防止了汇兑损失，甚至产生了套期保值利润。

4.2.3 外汇掉期交易

外汇掉期交易包含两笔同步的、不可分割的合同交易，一笔是即期交易，另一笔(与即期交易方向相反)是远期交易(在这种情况下外汇头寸结清了)。

或者，换句话说：同时购买和出售数额相同但期限不同的货币。

掉期可以有固定的期限：

- "隔夜掉期"(资金从交割日开始起息，第二天到期归还资金)。

- "明日掉期"(明日掉后日)。

- "次日掉期"(即期掉次日)。
- "7 天掉期"(周末掉期)。
- "1 个月(2 个月,3 个月,……)掉期"或者不规则交割日掉期:
  45 天,65 天,95 天。

4.2.4 期货交易

期货是在交易所而不是在场外证券市场进行的远期交易。为促进市场的流动性,期货交易的数量、交割日及标价都是标准化的。因为欧洲市场远期外汇业务效率高且更灵活使得外汇期货市场没能在欧洲建立起来,但利率期货却显示出了一定的重要性。过去几年中人们听到许多关于金融创新的说法,特别是关于标准化的期货合约。在这种背景下,美国期货交易所开发了大量的创新产品。大量的金融期货合约(金融期货)与传统的商品和金属远期交易(商品期货)一起出现在各类交易所。这些期货包括股票期货、利率期货、外汇期货和股票指数期货。从 1990 年 11 月 9 日开始,以瑞士市场指数为基础的股票指数期货合约在瑞士期权和金融期货交易所上市交易。在瑞士银行集团内,利率和货币期权通过纽约的 SBCI 期货交易所进行。

4.2.5 货币和利率期权

随着汇率制度(由固定汇率)过渡到浮动汇率,中央银行不再有义务将汇率保持在《布雷顿森林协议》所界定的狭窄范围内。持续的国际收支不平衡导致了汇率波动的加剧,特别是跨境资本流动放宽以后。因此如何消除货币风险变得极其紧迫。20 世纪 80 年代初创立的外汇期权,在减少汇率风险方面起了决定性的作用,并且相对于之前的外汇市场交易工具有更大的灵活性。

远期外汇交易中买卖双方确定了未来外汇交易的汇率,而期权交易中买方只有执行合约的权利,没有执行合约的义务,也就是说,买方可以执行期权合约,也可以不执行。因此通过外汇期权交易可以规避汇率损失,也可能获得收益。

以下是(欧式)期权的类型。

1. 买入期权(看涨期权)

在合约规定的到期日，买方有权按固定的汇率(即履约价格)购买一定数量的某种货币。

2. 卖出期权(看跌期权)

在合约规定的到期日，买方有权按固定的汇率(即履约价格)出售一定数量的某种货币。

需要指出这里的权利并不意味着有义务必须行使这一期权合约。

买方有权决定是购买还是出售合约规定数量的货币，为此他需要支付期权费。期权的卖方在两种情况下都没有选择，为此他可以获得买方结清合约必须支付的期权费。

4.3 外汇管制

外汇管制是指一国官方对外汇交易进行管制。管制的范围很广，包括进出口的货物和服务，汇出汇款，资金的流入及流出，汇率，付款方式，维持外汇交易中心的平衡，购买和持有的外国证券，居民和非居民的金融关系等。外汇管制限制人们把一国货币自由地兑换成另一国货币，从而使货币不可自由兑换。

大多数发展中国家进行外汇管制的主要目的是防止官方储备或本币对外价值的不利影响对国际收支产生的压力，以使国际收支平衡，确保贸易和资金的流向有助于其实现发展目标。

除了对商品的进出口进行管制，还有其他的外汇管制方法。

(1) 对于特定国家的港口和出口进行管制。

(2) 为了避免国际收支赤字而达成的双边协定。

一般由财政部负责实施外汇管制的法律、规章和外汇管制政策协调。外汇管制法规的具体执行往往委托给中央银行，但在许多情况下，这项工作分给若干部门或机构来对特定的国际交易进行管理。在我国，中国人民银行对外汇管制的法律和规章进行管理。在日常的外汇管制中，往往按照

Chapter 4　Foreign Exchange Markets

政府的外汇管制条例处理所有的外汇交易。而确保外币的收入和支出有合法有效的交易背景通常是银行的职责。

不同的国家有不同的外汇管制制度。大多数国家采用单一汇率制度，即所有的外汇交易都按照单一的官方汇率进行。单一汇率制度由外汇管制机构管理，它是外汇市场上唯一的买方和卖方。出口商和其他人收到外国居民的外汇必须按官方汇率出售给外汇管制当局。进口商和其他人必须获得许可才能按官方汇率从管制当局购买外汇进行对外支付。管制当局也可能对外国居民拥有的本币(银行账户)的使用进行规定。商业银行常常被授权作为管制当局的代理机构进行外汇的买卖。单一汇率制度通常配合进口配额、进口许可证和出口许可证制度使用。通常，进口许可证也可作为外汇许可证。但是，在一些国家除了进口许可证之外还需要外汇许可证。

Subject Topic(命题对话)

The Asian Financial Crisis
(亚洲金融危机)

A: The Asian financial crisis was the most important event in 1997 and 1998. I am very interested in this issue. I want to have a discussion with you about this event. To me, I think the outbreak of the Asian financial crisis in July 1997 resulted from the interaction among various internal and external factors in those countries.

B: Well, I would say the deterioration of their economic systems is the fundamental cause while the attack from international speculators sped it up.

A: I think the inappropriate pegged exchange rate system played a negative role in this event. It is such pegged exchange rate systems that touched off the crisis. For a long time, the Southeast Asian countries had fixed their currencies' exchange rates. Competitiveness had been weakened because of continuous deficit in their current accounts while the US economy has developed steadily. Under such conditions, to maintain the pegged exchange rate increased the pressure of devaluation on their currencies and made them vulnerable to attack from international speculation.

B: I think another reason is the imbalance of economic structure in these countries. During their economic booming period the Southeast Asian countries had invested a huge amount of capital in stocks and real estate rather than in the pillar industries. Therefore when economic growth slowed down, that investment only brought about large quantities of dead and uncollectible accounts.

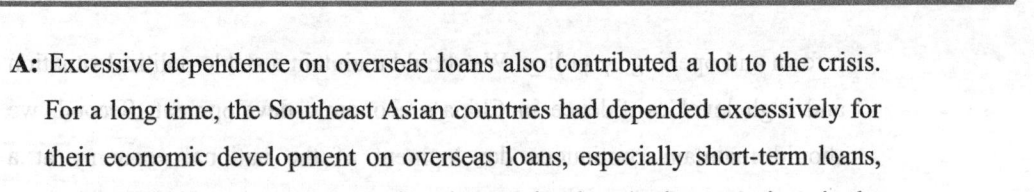

Chapter 4　Foreign Exchange Markets

A: Excessive dependence on overseas loans also contributed a lot to the crisis. For a long time, the Southeast Asian countries had depended excessively for their economic development on overseas loans, especially short-term loans, which brought to them a tremendous interest burden. At the same time, in the Southeast Asian countries, nearly no single country had a fiscal budget balance.

B: In addition, I think the Southeast Asian countries opened up their capital accounts when they had not yet set up complete financial, taxation and government budget systems. They had weak financial supervision on financial activities. The attacks from international speculators and the consequent capital flight further intensified the critical situation.

A: I remember the Mexican financial crisis in 1994. The main reason for the crisis was rapid trade liberalization and inappropriate foreign investment policy. I find that there are several similarities between the two crises, such as huge deficit in current account, inappropriate foreign investment policy, excessive dependence on foreign loans especially short-term loans, inappropriate foreign exchange policy, excessive opening up of financial markets, imbalance of economic structure and so on.

B: But there still remain some differences between them. I think the Asian financial crisis resulted from the deterioration of the internal economy and the crisis was speeded up by external attacks. However, in Mexico, it was the economic panic and the consequent capital flight that resulted from Mexico's default to its due debts that caused the financial crisis. Compared with the Mexican crisis, the Asian financial crisis has spread more widely and lasted longer.

A: What do you think we can learn from the Asian financial crisis?

B: I think the most important lesson is that economy and finance are closely linked. In order to maintain a sound economy so as to guarantee financial stability we have to do a lot of work. First of all, we should adhere to the reform and opening up policy. We should maintain a stable political situation and high level confidence in China's economic development. Second, we should maintain continuous development of the national economy at a moderately rapid level, improve the economic structure and increase the investment in infrastructure construction to support economic development. In addition, we should also speed up the reform of state-owned enterprises and enforce the macro-control and guard against the bubble economy.

A: Yes, and at the same time, we should also take efforts to improve China's financial area.

B: For example, I think we should adhere to a moderately tight financial and monetary policy. We should enforce financial supervision to guard against risks. On the other hand, we should speed up the transition of state-owned commercial banks to become real market-oriented commercial banks. Finally, we should open up the capital account gradually only when conditions permit and we should improve the foreign trade structure and maintain the balance in current accounts.

A: Well, we have discussed a lot about the crisis, but I still have a question. Since the outbreak of the Asian financial crisis in July 1997, the international community and the crisis-stricken countries have taken many measures to overcome the crisis. However, the Asian financial market is still in turmoil. What are the main reasons for that?

B: I think first of all, the slow and even negative economic growth caused by the crisis has hampered stability in Asia. Second, the devaluation of currencies has increased the debt burden for those enterprises in the crisis-stricken countries and accordingly reduced their production. Third, with the sharp increase in dead and uncollectible debts, banks in those countries have still been trapped in the plight.

A: Why is China safe from the economic crisis in Asia?

B: China enjoys a stable political situation and achieves continuous surplus in its

Chapter 4   Foreign Exchange Markets

current and capital accounts. Besides, China's foreign debts are mainly long-term loans and China possesses up to US$140 billion in foreign exchange reserves. This offers China strong resistance to the economic crisis. At the same time, China has not opened up its capital account and has still imposed strict restriction on the inflow of hot money. However, it does not mean that there exist no problems in China's financial field. The problems related to debts owned by state-owned enterprises to state-owned commercial banks has been quite serious. The transition for sate-owned commercial banks to become genuine market-oriented commercial banks has made very slow progress.

Questions and Answers(专业问答)

1. What is exchange rate? What are the two marked price methods?
    —The exchange rate refers to the price of one currency expressed in terms of another. And there are two marked price methods are used. They are direct and indirect methods.

2. Which currencies use indirect marked price method?
    —GBP, AUD, NZD and ECU use indirect marked price method.

3. Which marked price method does Euro use?
    —It uses indirect price method.

4. Which characteristics does foreign exchange have?
    —It is payable, accessible and convertible.

5. Which factors decide the change of exchange rate?
    —They are international payment, inflation and expectations.

6. What are spot exchange rates? What are forward exchange rates?
    —Spot exchange rates are rates that are quoted for spot transaction of foreign exchange. Spot transactions usually require delivery of the

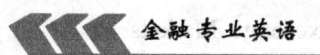

exchange involved within two business days.

Forward exchange rates are fixed at the time the contract is opened and the contract is firm and binding upon both parties's delivery or sale at an agreed time in future.

7. What is the full name of LIBOR?

——It is London Inter-bank Offering Rate.

Exercises(练习)

Reading Comprehension

Passage One

A foreign exchange transaction may be described as a contract to exchange a bank balance in one currency with a bank in another currency at an agreed rate of exchange at specified point of time; the three main user groups of foreign exchange market are banks, brokers and customers.

Banks participate in the inter-bank market to move large sums of money around. The underlying purpose of these transactions may be to meet some form of customer requirement for currency, perhaps as a result of a trade finance transaction or because the customer wishes to create an investment position or hedge some existing position.

For the accounting of foreign exchange, it is necessary to define a few terms as follows:

- Natural currency: Natural currency is the actual currency of the transaction.
- Local currency: Local currency is the currency in use in the country of operation.
- Foreign currency: Foreign currency is any currency other than local

Chapter 4 Foreign Exchange Markets

currency in the country of operation.

- Local currency equivalent: Local currency equivalent is any currency translated into the local currency.

- Base currency: The base currency is only used for reporting purposes. It may, for example, be the currency of the organization's parent.

Two accounting systems can generally be used to account for foreign exchange transactions, namely, the dual currency accounting system and the multiple currency accounting system.

In dual currency accounting system, all ledgers are maintained in local currency, with foreign currency transactions being recorded in local currency equivalents.

In the multiple currency accounting system, all foreign currency transactions are only in the natural currency, a separate currency ledger being maintained for each currency used. For cross currency transactions, which involve two currencies and therefore two separate ledgers, offset entries are posted to separate control accounts utilized for each currency. This is the most widely used basis for accounting for foreign currency.

1. If the British branch of an American bank is selling Australian dollars to a German bank, the natural currency is _____.

    A. US dollar

    B. Australian dollar

    C. British Pounds

    D. Euro

2. Two accounting systems can generally be used to account for foreign exchange transactions, namely, _____.

    A. the single entry system and double entry system

    B. the single entry system and the multiple currency accounting system

C. the double entry system and the multiple currency accounting system

D. None of the above is true.

3. In dual currency accounting system, all ledgers are maintained_____.

A. in foreign currency, with foreign currency transactions being recorded in local currency equivalents

B. in natural currency, with foreign currency transactions being recorded in local currency equivalents

C. in local currency, with foreign currency transactions being recorded in local currency equivalents

D. in base currency, with foreign currency transactions being recorded in local currency equivalents

4. If the British branch of an American bank is selling Australian dollars to a German bank, local currency equivalent is_____.

A. Australian dollars expressed as British Pounds

B. Australian dollars expressed as American dollars

C. British Pounds expressed as Australian dollars

D. American dollars expressed as Australian dollars

5. In the multiple currency accounting system, all foreign currency transactions are only in _____.

A. local currency, and a separate entry being maintained for each currency used

B. natural currency, and a separate ledger maintained for each currency used

C. base currency, and a double entry being maintained for each currency used

D. foreign currency, and a separate currency ledger being maintained for each currency used

Chapter 4 Foreign Exchange Markets

Passage Two

Foreign exchange receipts of domestic entities for current account transactions shall be repatriated home and shall not be deposited abroad. Foreign exchange receipts for current account transactions shall be sold to the designated foreign exchange banks in accordance with the regulations issued by the State Council on the sale, purchase, and payment of foreign exchange, or be deposited in the foreign exchange account upon approval. Foreign exchange for current account payment and transfers may be purchased from designated foreign exchange banks upon the presentation of valid documents and commercial bills.

After the foreign exchange restrictions on current account transactions were lifted in 1996, cases of fraud of foreign exchange have increased significantly. To address such problems, the SAFE has taken enforcement actions. To enforce the surrender of export proceeds, the SAFE and its local branches undertake to verify collection of export earnings. When exporting goods abroad, domestic exporting entities are required to undergo the verification procedures. The customs offices shall accept and handle declaration for export based on verification certificate within validity period. Only after no mistakes are found in the examination can customs permit entrance and clearance. After goods have been shipped out of Chinese territory, the customs shall write their opinion and stamp with "proof seal" on the verification certificate, with which the exporter goes through verification procedures. The exporter must send the stub of verification certificate together with commercial invoices and declaration form to the SAFE within 60 days from the date of customs declaration. The export earnings are then surrendered to designated banks or entered the exporter's foreign exchange account.

1. Foreign exchange receipts of domestic companies for current account goods_____.

    A. shall be sent home or deposited abroad

B. shall be sold to the designated foreign exchange banks in accordance with relevant regulations

C. might be deposited in the foreign exchange account upon approval

D. Both B and C

2. If domestic entities need foreign exchange for current account payment,_____.

A. they can buy it from any foreign exchange banks

B. they can buy it from the designated foreign exchange banks unconditionally

C. they can buy it from the designed foreign exchange banks by showing the relevant valid commercial documents

D. they can buy it from any banks by presenting valid documents and commercial bills

3. The removal of the foreign exchange restrictions on current account transactions _____.

A. has restrained fraud in foreign exchange business

B. adds to the chances of the fraud of foreign exchange

C. would mean fraud activity in foreign exchange will be easier to be identified

D. would mean there will be no fraud of foreign exchange

4. When exporting goods abroad, domestic exporting entities are required_____.

A. to go through the verification procedures

B. to go through the customs clearance process

C. to send the stub of verification certificate together with commercial invoices and declaration form to the SAFE within 60 days from the date of customs declaration

D. All of the above

Chapter 4　Foreign Exchange Markets

5.　The export earning will be_____.

A. purchased from the designated banks by the exporters

B. submitted to the designated banks or entered into the exporter's foreign exchange account

C. deposited in any bank

D. deposited in any domestic bank

Part II Financial Institutions and Their Operations

- Chapter 5 Commercial Banking
- Chapter 6 Investment Banking
- Chapter 7 Insurance
- Chapter 8 Securities

Chapter 5
Commercial Banking

5.1 Intermediary Services

Functions performed by commercial banks are:
1) creation of money through lending and investing activities;
2) holding of the deposits;
3) provision of a mechanism for payment and transfer of funds.

Intermediary services of commercial banks cover International Settlement, Trust Services, Lease and Factoring.

5.1.1 Relationship between Banks and Customers

1. Debtor-Creditor Relationship

It arises out of the fact that the bank holds money that belongs to the customer. The money has to be repaid at some time, and therefore the bank is the debtor, while the customer is the creditor.

As for the bank's intermediary services, it is not referring to those lending and borrowing activities, i.e., the relationship between a banker and its customers is not debtor-creditor one. The relationship between a banker and its client as intermediary services is a principal-agent one, i.e. the bank is acting as an agent for its client.

2. Principal-Agent Relationship

A bank, when dealing with its customer directly, has a debtor-creditor

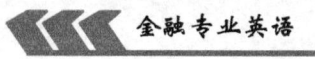金融专业英语

relationship. But where a third party is involved the relationship becomes one of that between a principal and an agent.

Agreement: one party (agent) agrees to act on behalf of the other party (principal). Agents have the authority to perform legal acts for the principal with the agency agreement.

Principal's obligations: 1) compensate the agent according to the agreement; 2) reimburse the agent for reasonable expenses; 3) indemnify the agent against loss or liability for duties performed on behalf of the principal and 4) inform the agent of risks.

Agent's obligations: 1) act in the best interest of the principal and with complete loyalty; 2) carry out the instruction of the principal with reasonable care and skills; 3) account to the principal; 4) indemnify the principal for damages wrongfully caused to the principal and 5) provide information to the principal.

5.1.2 Items of Intermediary Services

1. Settlement

Settlement is the striking of a balance between two or more parties having dealings with one another.

The evolution of the settlement goes through three stages: Cash-based, Paper-based and Electronic-based. Also, Negotiable Instruments such as Bills of Exchange, Cheques and Promissory Notes are wildly used as instruments in the international settlement. They represent a right to payment. A right is a promise and not a tangible piece of property. So, they are classified as chooses in action.

2. Trust Services

Individuals or corporations may desire a reliable outside entity to administer their assets. Banks offer trust services to meet this need.

Trust Service: is a fiduciary relationship in which one person is trusted by

Chapter 5 Commercial Banking

the holder of the legal title to property, subject to an obligation to keep or use the property for the benefit of the holder. There are three parties involving in the operation of Trust Service: a. the trustor, b. the beneficiary, c. the trustee.

3. Lease

It is a contract granting the possession of lands, tenements, buildings, office, machinery or other chattels for a specified fixed period. Since the possession and use of the property is conveyed by owner to the user in a lease, the property reverts to the owner at the end of the term.

4. Factoring

Factoring is short-term financing from the nonrecourse sale of accounts receivable to a third party.

5.2 International Settlement

5.2.1 Remittance

Remittance refers to the transfer of funds from one party to another among different countries through banks. At the request of its customer, a bank transfers a certain sum of money to its overseas branches or correspondent banks and instructs them to pay a named person or corporation in that country.

1. Means or Instruments of Remittance

The remittance will be done by several means or instruments such as mail transfer, demand draft and telegraphic transfer. The instruments mentioned above bear their characteristics, which will be discussed later.

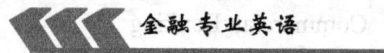金融专业英语

2. Mail Transfer(M/T)

A mail transfer is to transfer funds by means of a payment order or a mail advice, or sometimes a debit advice issued by a remitting bank, at the request of a remitter. Either of a payment order, mail advice or debit advice must be authenticated with tested key or the authorized signatures of the remitting bank. It instructs the paying bank to pay a certain sum of money to the beneficiary. Upon receipt of the payment order, the paying bank verifies the tested key or the authorized signature, notifies the beneficiary, pays to him and claims reimbursement from the remitting bank. In practice, the remitting bank credits the account for the paying bank in the remitting bank.

3. Demand Draft(D/D)

Draft demand is often used when the customer wants to transfer the funds to his beneficiary by himself. The remitter will make a written request of issuance to the remitting bank. Then the remitting bank debits the remitter's account, issues a bank draft and forwards it to the remitter who may send or carry it abroad to the payee. Upon receipt of the draft, the payee can either present it for payment to the drawee's bank or sell it to his own bank crediting his account. The drawee's bank verifies the signature, pays the draft and claims back the amount paid in accordance with its agency arrangement with the remitting bank.

4. Telegraphic Transfer (T/T)

Telegraphic transfer refers to remittance by Swift. It is exactly the same as a mail transfer, except that instruction from the remitting bank to the paying bank is transmitted by cable/telex/Swift instead of by mail. Therefore, it is faster, but more expensive than the mail transfer. It is often used when the remittance amount is large and the transfer of funds is subject to a time limit. Thus 90%

Chapter 5   Commercial Banking

remittance is done through T/T.

5.2.2   Documentary Collections

1. Procedures

A documentary collection is an operation in which a bank collects payment on behalf of the seller (the principal) by delivering documents to the buyer.

Documentary collections are very suitable in cases where the exporter is reluctant to supply the goods on an open account basis but does not need the degree of security provided by a documentary credit. A documentary collection gives greater security than settlement on open account, because the importer cannot take possession of the goods without either making payment or accepting a bill of exchange. The banks concerned are under no obligation to pay.

In a documentary collection the exporter cannot be sure at the time of dispatch of the goods that the buyer will actually pay the sum owed. This form of settlement is therefore most appropriate in the following cases:

- if the exporter has no doubt about the buyer's willingness and ability to pay;
- if the political, economic and legal environment in the importing country is considered to be stable;
- if the buyer's country has placed no restrictions on imports (e.g. exchange controls) or has issued all the necessary authorizations.

2. Stages of a Documentary Collection

The whole process, extending from the first contact between the importer and exporter to the completion of the transaction, can involve many separate steps. Basically, however, a documentary collection has three stages:

STAGE 1   Establishing the terms of collection

The exporter stipulates the terms of payment in his offer or agrees them with the buyer in the contract of sale.

85

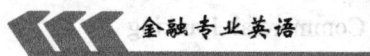金融专业英语

STAGE 2　Collection order and transmission of documents

After the contract of sale has been signed, the exporter dispatches the goods direct to the buyer. At the same time, he assembles all the necessary documents (invoice, bill of lading, insurance certificate, certificate of origin, etc.) and sends them to his own bank (the remitting bank) together with the collection order. The remitting bank then sends the documents, together with the necessary instructions, to the collecting bank.

STAGE 3　Presentation of documents and settlement

The collecting bank informs the buyer of the arrival of the documents and notifies him of the terms of their release. The buyer makes payment, or accepts of exchange, and in return receives the documents. The collecting bank then transfers the collected amount to the remitting bank, which credits it to the exporter's account.

3. Participants

There are usually four parties to a documentary collection operation:

- exporter (seller, principal)
- remitting bank
- collecting bank; the term 'collecting bank' is applied to any bank, which is involved in the execution of the collection order, and it presents the documents to the importer.
- importer (buyer, drawee)

4. Establishing the Terms of Collection

An exporter has been invited by a prospective foreign buyer to submit an offer for the supply of goods.

A. Documents against payment (D/P)

The presenting bank is authorized to release the documents to the drawee only against immediate payment. In international usage, 'immediate' means 'no

86

Chapter 5   Commercial Banking

later than the arrival of the goods'.

B. Documents against acceptance (D/A)

The presenting bank releases the documents to the importer against his acceptance of a bill of exchange, which is usually payable 30-180 days after sight or at a fixed future date.

5. Collection Order

When making out the collection order, special attention should be paid to the following points: Buyer's address, Type of collection, Documents, Name and address of presenting bank, Bill of exchange, Commissions and expenses, Case-of-need, Special remarks, Bank account and Signature.

6. Forwarding the Documents to the Collecting Bank

The remitting bank sends the documents, together with the necessary instructions, to a bank in the buyer's country.

Costs of collection are low and the customer gets good value for money. The bank places at his disposal not only the services of its own experienced specialists but also a worldwide network of contacts, which ensures that payments, documents and information are transmitted safely and reliably even in exceptional situations.

5.2.3 Documentary Credit

1. Principles and Characteristics

The letter of credit has been created in order to provide an instrument to international trade offering security to the exporter, as far as payment is concerned, and security to the importer enabling him to pay against documents which can prove that the goods ordered have been shipped in good order and in conformity to the commercial contract.

The Uniform Customs and Practices provide some basic principles: the

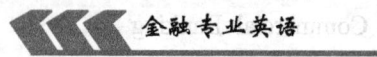

autonomy of the documentary credit and the documentary credit deals with documents, not with goods.

2. Operation of Documentary Credit

According to UCP rules banks dealing in letters of credit only deal with documents and not with goods. Therefore banks should only consider documents being in conformity with credit terms on their face.

This means as it says that banks should scrutinize documents with reasonable care and look for any discrepancy between documents and letter of credit as well as between documents amongst themselves.

L/C business is in the first place an interbank business where the advising/confirming bank relies on the standing of the irrevocable and unconditional undertaking of the issuing bank. This also includes the professional skills of the issuing bank. It is obvious that the issuing bank has the same professional expectations of the advising/confirming bank. Otherwise it would have chosen an other bank to channel its credits.

By issuing a L/C the bank engages itself towards a colleague by taking a credit risk on the applicant. Once issued it does not matter the evolution of the credit worthiness of the applicant or the state or the price evolution of goods. The undertaking is an independent and final one.

As said before the reason for refusing documents because of minor discrepancies is very often inspired by the buyer wanting to control the goods before payment or because the buyer already received the goods and experienced them as not being in conformity with the order.

Of course the more detailed documents are prescribed in the L/C, the more discrepancies can occur by presenting non conform documents. Bankers should, based on their experience, advise the customer about the right way to choose the documents and how to prescribe them.

Examining documents with a reasonable care is not only the duty of the

Chapter 5   Commercial Banking

banks to protect their customer but is also their duty against their partner banker in the L/C. By examining documents and drawing the attention of the issuing bank on discrepancies, advising/confirming banks may prevent payments by the former mislead by the wording "conform documents presented". Indeed when afterward documents arriving at the issuing bank present discrepancies which have not been informed, the issuing bank and/or applicant might have troubles to recover the money already paid. It might also be that the buyer/applicant will not have any recourse any more.

Finally, any bank has to draw the immediate attention of his partner banker in the L/C if their is any suspicion of fraud or fraudulent activity which might limit the other party's rights.

When finding discrepancies the issuing bank should not fail to inform the remitting bank within a reasonable time. In the new UCP this means within 7 working days. In other words, the issuing bank should send a message to the remitting bank the seventh working day at the latest informing about the discrepancies and telling documents are held at the disposal of the remitting bank pending further instructions. One should also bear in mind that all discrepancies found be mentioned at the same time and that it is unacceptable to mention additional discrepancies later on by a following message.

3. Fraud in Documentary Credit

Both characteristics of documentary credits, the autonomy and the documentary base, can also be used in criminal actions. As the international businessman uses documentary credits as security to receive payment against presentation only of conform documents and as the issuing bank undertakes to pay against presentation only of conform documents, without having to be involved in the execution of the underlying contract, some criminals have set up systems to fraud against innocent business men and banks. They turned the documentary credit into an instrument of making money easily.

89

- Fake documents can be presented under real credits.
- Fake documentary credits can be issued in favour of innocent beneficiaries.
- Fantastic drafts of documentary credits.

All systems might be used to commit fraud and/or in view of money laundering. They may also appear as commercial documentary credit or as stand-letter of credit.

False documents tendered under real documentary credits are rare but difficult to discover. Most criminals in this business are real specialists and will tender perfectly falsified documents. Fraud is mostly discovered by skilled bank staff through executing some basic cross checks. Be aware of unknown beneficiaries presenting perfect documents under documentary credits for large amounts and asking for immediate payment.

Fake documentary credits are easier to discover. They mainly seem to have been issued in African countries but more and more some are appearing coming Eastern-European countries or non-existing countries. They look like originals and can only be discovered by looking into very small details.

If a beneficiary receives a documentary credit straight from an issuing bank, without being advised by a local bank there is a doubt about fraud. First of all he should go and see his banker and ask to check the authenticity before starting to manufacture or dispatch anything. He should certainly not start to issue guarantees.

The technique is often used to attract innocent people looking into high yield investments and who will loose their money as never being reimbursed and simultaneously this kind of letters of credit will be used for money laundering.

Once again fraud often try to have the names of first class banks involved to attract other innocent investors or bankers.

Chapter 5　Commercial Banking

5.2.4　Guarantees

1. Types of Guarantees

There are several types of guarantees which the seller may be called upon to provide in favour of the buyer. The most common types are:

(1) Bid bonds or tender guarantees

Sellers are often required to submit a guarantee with their tender for a contract, commonly for an amount between 2% and 5% of the offered price. The purpose of a tender guarantee is to promise payment in case the beneficiary stated that the tender has changed the conditions of his tender or has withdrawn his tender during the binding period or that he did not sign the contract although he got the award.

(2) Performance guarantees

They are the most commonly used types of guarantees and may be required even though no other type of guarantee is necessary.

Performance guarantees usually contain an undertaking to pay a certain sum, commonly between 5% and 10% of the contract value, if the buyer claims that the seller has failed to perform the terms of the contract. It would be normal for a performance guarantee to replace any tender guarantee which may have been issued in order to get the contract. In case the underlying contract prescribes some obligations to be secured by a guarantee e.g. delivery, warrant, erection, etc., the performance guarantee may be restricted accordingly.

(3) Down or advance payment guarantees

Under the terms of the contract an advance payment is offered to meet the sellers mobilization or other initial costs. This type of guarantee is normally required as security for the repayment in case of non contractual delivery. The amount of an advance payment is commonly between 10% and 20% of the contract price and it is desirable for these guarantees if possible to be written in

91

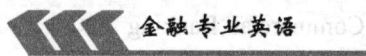

a form that makes them effective only upon receipt by the seller of agreed advance payment. It is also quite common for these guarantees to contain a reduces pro rata of delivered goods upon presentation to the bank of copies of shipping documents. Another reduction can be formulated for the case completion of work on site, to be evidenced by presentation to the bank of specified completion certificates. It is most important that the terms of the guarantee make clear how reductions in liability are to be effected.

(4) Retention money guarantees

Some contracts provide for a percentage of each payment up to 10% to be withheld until the project has been completed and accepted by the buyer, alternatively the retention can be paid to sellers against a retention money guarantee. That guarantee secures seller's compliance with his warranty obligations and enables the buyer to release the retained amount before termination of the warranty period.

(5) Maintenance guarantees

Maintenance guarantees are normally requested in connection with construction contracts. The purpose of a maintenance guarantee is to secure the constructor's obligations during the maintenance period once the construction has been completed. Such guarantees may also be issued in lieu of retaining money for the maintenance period.

2. First Demand Bank Guarantees

First demand bank guarantees are legally bound by obligations on the bank for which the bank will need to be indemnified by the seller. They may provide for payment on first demand against beneficiary's statement of non fulfillment of a specified contractual liability. On the other hand that guarantees may promise payment upon first demand, plus beneficiary's statement and presentation of documents referred to in the guarantee. This means that, if a bank receives a demand which on its face complied with the terms of the guarantee the bank must pay and will pay without any objections of its customer.

Guarantees calling for independently produced documents e.g. certificate of an arbitration award or a copy of forwarding agents certificate of receipt may be regarded as "Conditional Guarantee".

Nowadays, the necessary independence of the bank guarantee from the underlying transaction is emphasized world-wide by using the clause "to pay on first demand". This clause covers the waiver of all protests and objections in connection with that transaction.

Improper calls upon the guarantor can be prevented by making timely arrangements, i.e. in the purchase contract, that further documentary evidence of the default is to be presented when calling upon the guarantor. Certificates from public authorities, independent expert opinions, declarations signed by both the importer and exporter, arbitration awards and similar documents would be acceptable. It is important that one of these documents be described in as much detail as for a documentary credit, clearly showing reference to that contract for which the guarantee has been issued.

The abstract nature of the guarantee is not jeopardized by the mere stipulation that the beneficiary, when claiming payments, must present documents which are adequately and unambiguously defined in the guarantee.

3. Direct Guarantees

Exporter's bank issues its declaration in favour of the foreign beneficiary to whom the deed will be sent by the guarantor, by the client on collection basis or under letter of credit. In case of implementation the beneficiary is asked to lodge his claim via his bankers in order to have them approve the correctness of signatures appearing on the claim.

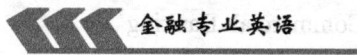

4. Indirect Guarantees

Exporter's bank instructs a foreign correspondent bank to issue the respective guarantee in favour of a beneficiary under its counterguarantee by which exporter's bank stands surety towards the foreign bank. Normally a counterguarantee is payable on first demand of the foreign bank stating that it has been requested by beneficiaries to make payment under its guarantee.

Naturally, the indirect guarantee is more problematic than the direct one as a foreign bank is added to the chain of parties involved in the guarantee. The foreign bank's guarantee is subject to the law in force at the lieu of issue and all consequences arising thereof are to be born by the instructing bank and its customers.

5.2.5　Standby Letter of Credit

A "standby letter of credit", is an instrument similar to a guarantee, by means of which payment(s) and/or performance are guaranteed, e.g. repayment of a loan or the delivery of goods according to contract or fulfillment of works/contracts. The standby letter of credit is designed to indemnify the beneficiary in the event of opening bank's client to fail in complying with his commitments arising out of the underlying contract.

Standby letters of credit may include (1) performance bond guarantees, in which a bank guarantees that a building or other project will be completed on time, or (2) default guarantees, under which a bank pledges the repayment of defaulted corporate notes and state and local government bonds when the borrowers cannot pay. These standby letters enable borrowing customers to get the credit they require at lower cost and on more flexible terms. In order to sell these guarantees successfully, however, the bank must have a higher credit rating than its customer. Because many U.S. banks have experienced declines in their credit ratings in recent years, their competitors (including foreign banks

Chapter 5   Commercial Banking

and insurance companies) have recently moved in to capture a large share of the credit guarantee market.

A standby credit letters is a contingent obligation of the letter's issuer. The issuing bank or non-bank firm, in return for a fee, agrees to guarantee the credit of its customer or to guarantee the fulfillment of a contract made by its customer with a third party. The key advantages to a bank issuing standbys are the following:

(1) Letter of credit earn the bank a fee for providing the service (usually around 0.5 percent to 1 percent of the amount of credit involved).

(2) They aid a customer, who can usually borrow more cheaply when armed with the bank's guarantee, without using up the bank's scarce reserves.

(3) Such guarantees usually can be issued at relatively low cost because the issuing bank may already know the financial condition of its standby credit customer (e.g., when that customer applied for his or her last loan).

(4) The probability is low that the issuer of the credit guarantee will ever be called upon to pay.

5.3   Credit Loan

5.3.1 Commercial Loans

By maturity, loans can be divided into two broad categories. Those with maturity of one year or less are called short-term loans while these with maturity exceeding one year called medium or long-term loans. Short-term loans are often used to satisfy working capital needs whereas medium and long-term loans are often used to finance fixed asset investment. Loans can also be categorized according to the nature of contractual arrangement as well as intended use.

5.3.2 Special Credit

1. Export Credit

Export Credit is government (government export credit agencies) guarantee lending channeled though a commercial bank to support export. There are two kinds of export credit: buyer credit and supplier credit.

In buyer credit, exporter's bank provides loans to the importer (importer's bank guarantees) or to importer's bank, which on-lends the loan to the importer. Importers can obtain loan to meet their needs of purchasing exporters' goods. A buyer credit usually includes the following terms and conditions:

- Loan is arranged in support of a supply contract for capital goods and related service mainly from the country to provide loan.

- Value of financing is available for 85% of the eligible contract value. The balance must be paid in cash or with a commercial loan.

- Period of financing varies with each contract considered to be eligible and approved for financing, normally between 5 and 10 years.

- Payment of financing should be in equal half yearly installment of principle commencing from a time determined by the export credit agency or the scopes of the supply contract.

- Interest rate is fixed in accordance with OECD monthly according to market interest rates and return rates of treasury bills.

- Commitment fee at a rate per annum is calculated from the date of signing of the loan agreement until the date of full disbursement of the loan thereunder on the amount of loan not disbursed from time to time.

- Management fee is calculated at flat on the amount of the loan.

- Credit insurance premiums as determined by agencies are payable by the borrow or added to the supply contract value and refinanced under

Chapter 5 Commercial Banking

the term of the export credit loan.

The procedure of buyer credit varies depending on whether the importer's bank provides guarantee or on-lends it when the loan is provided to the importer. In the first case, the follow procedures are followed:

- Exporter's bank and importer's bank conclude a general agreement (frame agreement) of export credit. Importer's bank requires and exporter's bank agrees to make available the Facility Line pursuant to the term and conditions of the agreement.
- The exporter and the importer conclude a supply contract.
- The exporter and the importer make an application to exporter's bank and importer's bank respectively.
- Exporter's bank signs an individual loan agreement with the importer's bank to finance the export credit agency, and the loan agreement comes into effect after the export credit agency has approved it.

In the second case, the following procedures are applied:

- The exporter and the importer conclude a supply contract.
- The exporter and the importer make an application to exporter's bank and importer's bank respectively.
- Export's bank signs a loan agreement with the importer, and importer's bank issues a letter of guarantee in favor of exporter's bank after they accept the applications respectively.
- Exporter's bank make an application for the individual loan agreement to government's export credit agency, and the loan agreement comes into effect after the export credit agency approves it.

The other export credit is supplier credit, In supplier credit, exporter's bank provides loans to the supplier (exporter) to finance the contract with special payment terms which importer pays for the contract goods by half yearly installments. Such terms require the issuance of bill of exchange be supplier for

pre-acceptance by the buyer /borrower. The usual terms and condition of supplier credit are the same as those of buyer credit. Supplier credit procedures are as follows:

- The supplier (exporter) enters into a contract with the importer for supplying goods and services. The payment terms of the contract requires the importer to pay for the goods in half yearly installment.

- The supplier and the importer apply to supplier's bank and importer's bank respectively. Importer's bank issues a letter of guarantee in favor of the supplier after accepting the application. Supplier's bank enters into a loan agreement with the supplier. The loan agreement and the contract come into effect after the export credit agency approves them.

2. Forfaiting

Forfaiting provides a source of non-recourse finance through use of drafts, promissory notes or other instruments representing sums due to the exporter. In essence, a bank in the seller's country (also called seller's bank, supplier's bank or exporter's bank) discounts a note or draft (bill) carrying the backing of the buyer's bank (also called a bank in buyer's country). Its main use is for short or medium-term financing for the export of capital goods. The term "forfaiting" is derived from the French "à forfait", which means to surrender or relinquish rights.

The basic mechanics of forfaiting are as follows. Typically, the buyer makes a down payment of 15-20 percent of the price. The balance is financed through the forfaiting market. The seller gets the same kind of security that he would obtain from confirmed letter of credit, because a bank in his own country commits itself in advance to pay him without recourse if he presents the appropriate documents.

Documentary credit is used where payment is immediate, or very short-term credit is being granted. Forfaiting provides an arrangement for larger

Chapter 5　Commercial Banking

sales being financed on a medium-term basis.

Forfaiting banks require the institution to have a guarantee by an internationally recognized bank. This reduces the risk and makes it easier to re-sell the draft or promissory note in the secondary market.

Forfaiting deals are carried out in a limited number of currencies. The most common currencies are US dollars, Euros and Swiss francs. This reduces the exchange risks for banks to commit themselves ahead.

The cost of the operation varies with the level of interest rates for currency at the time of the forfaiter's commitment, his assessment of the credit risk of the importing country, and the bank guaranteeing the paper.

The discounting bank works out the interest that it would have gained on the money. This is usually based on the cost of funds in the Euro market. It adds a charge to compensate for political risk and transfer risk attaching to the guaranteeing bank.

There is a secondary market of forfaiting deals in discounting paper, although it is a small one, available only to a few professional forfaiters. Risk is relatively high, and investors need to have capital recourse. Returns in this secondary market are higher than on much other equivalent investment.

Forfaiting procedures are as follows:

- The seller draws a bill of exchange (draft) on the buyer, who accepts it for payment at maturity. Alternatively the buyer issues a promissory note in favor of the seller. The date of payment in either case ties in with the credit terms granted to the buyer. In the majority cases payment is made by installments over the credit period. A series of drafts or notes with appropriate maturity dates is then issued.

- The bill is guaranteed by a bank in the buyer's country, and sent to the seller. The exporter can obtain immediate cash payment by discounting it with the forfaiting bank in his country. He endorse it to the bank on non-recourse terms. The bank is willing to agree to this because it has the security of guarantee given in the importer's country. The discount rate takes the extra risk of waiving recourse into account. In exceptional cases a forfaiter might be prepared to take papers not guaranteed by a bank. This is likely only if the importer has the best risk rating and there are no payment problems with the country concerned.

- Before the sales deal is finalized both parties check that their respective banks are willing to cooperate. The exporter gets his or her bank to quote its discount rate for the paper to be issued. Typically, banks are willing to commit themselves for up to a year or occasionally 18 months ahead. The exporter has to pay a commitment fee for a firm undertaking.

- The bill is issued for an amount that will give the exporter the agreed sales price (less than cash payment made by the importer) when the bank pays him the discounted value. Alternatively, it is issued for a lower value if the seller has agreed to take part of the finance cost as an incentive by the deal.

- The forfaiting bank obtains payment directly from the importer on the agreed maturity date. The buyer pays the full face value of the paper, which represents the sales price plus the bank's charge for the credit terms granted to the importer. The net result is the same as if the buyer had obtained a loan at the prevailing interest rate from the forfaiting bank.

Case Study

Your customer (exporting company with a yearly turnover of CHF 15m) is trying to conclude a delivery contract regarding the supply of textile machinery to a state-owned company in country XYZ. The contract value amounts to CHF 5m, the delivery period is max. 24 months, The tender documents are stating that the offer for the supplies must be accompanied by a financing offer.

Chapter 5   Commercial Banking

Preliminary investigations with the ECA showed, that the transaction would be covered with a cover-rate of 95%.

Your client is interested in a classical export financing (i.e. a normal sharing of the non-ECA covered risks) and submits the respective financing application form to you.

Questions:

(1) Can you offer an export financing?

(2) What considerations do you have to include into your credit decision?

(3) What is the amount of the Export loan?

Solutions:

(1) An offer for an export financing is in principle possible.

(2) Investigations/Clarifications/Considerations:

a. Is the exporter able to fulfill his contractual obligations with regard to the delivery period?

b. Is the exporter able to carry out such a large contract?

- past export experience?
- export %-age/turnover?
- major exporting countries?
- dependent on sub-supplier(s)?
- tailor made machines or standard product?
- experienced in working with country XYZ?

c. Does this client have limits available with your bank for

- bid bond?
- Down payment guarantee?
- Performance bond?
- Required pre-export financing?
- Recourse for the non-ECA covered risks?

d. Is there a letter of credit for the advance/intermediate payment? If so,

101

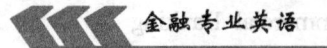

- to be opened through your bank (cross-selling possibility).
- is L/C to be confirmed by your bank (do you have limits for the L/C opening bank)?

(3) CHF 4.75m

5.3.3 Syndication

1. The Concept of Syndicated Loan

A syndicated loan is a loan arranged by a lead bank between a borrower, itself, and a group of other banks that are parties to the original credit agreement. These syndicate banks share credit information and credit risk.

A syndicated loan is a large credit, generally more than USD10 million, negotiated between a borrower and a single bank, but actually funded by several other banks. The negotiating or "lead" bank has often won the "mandate" from a number of competitors and has often underwritten a large portion of the credit and is responsible for organizing the syndication which includes inviting other banks to act as manager/ co-manager in providing additional underwriting support to the credit before going to market for general syndication to "participants". The resulting credit is governed by a single loan agreement signed by the borrower and all of the banks involved.

The syndication market has developed largely because single lenders have found it increasingly difficult to meet large borrowing requirements of corporate clients. Since syndication is usually arranged for sums ranging from USD 10 million to USD billion plus, a single bank may not be able or willing to extend such a large amount because of legal lending limits, exposure, and portfolio considerations. Also, the lead bank often chooses to allow room in its credit availability for future funding opportunities to the same borrower.

Every syndication has an agent bank to administer the loans from signing to repayment. Based on the complexity of its duties, the agent bank normally

Chapter 5   Commercial Banking

receives a fee from the borrower. This fee is separate and distinct from any front end or other fee paid to the bank. Duties of the agent bank include issuing advices for interest charges, processing the movement of funds, and assuring that the borrower has complied with the terms and conditions of the loan agreement.

2. Purpose of Syndicated Loan

The purpose of the syndicated loan is usually to finance a major development, a project, a temporary imbalance of payments, a major capital investment program, a project cost over-run, acquisition of a company, short-term to long-term debt conversion, or rationalization of its schedule of long-term debt repayments.

The most successful lead managers (banks) or co-lead managers in the syndication field are professionally adaptable at performing the four basic functions in a syndication, namely information memorandum preparation, documentation, syndication function and agency function. Information Memorandum, to be distributed to potential participants, presents detailed analysis of the borrower, including disclosures of the borrower's past performance, projections, management and an economic analysis of the borrower's country.

Lead manager bears potential obligation of preventing the memorandum from fraudulent or negligent misrepresentation. It should be emphasized that the borrower has warranted and confirmed that all information is true, accurate, complete and correct and that no independent verification or judgment is given by the managers. The lead manager, in conjunction with local and international legal assistance, prepares and negotiates an acceptable loan agreement and any necessary supplemental documentation. Documentation will naturally be acceptable to all participant levels in the syndication.

To perform the syndication function, the successful lead manager, in having secured a mandate from the borrower based on specific terms and

103

conditions, must market the loan to international financial institutions in a manner that is consistent with its selldown objective. This function is inherent portion of the loan. An in-depth understanding of the market and the borrower enables the lead manager to secure a mandate based on conditions which are acceptable in the market given the competitive aspects of securing mandates today. This is the most difficult and perilous function in loan syndication today.

Acting as an agent, the lead manager will oversee the loan throughout its tenor and act as an advisor for both the borrower and participants about condition precedent, representation and warranties.

5.3.4　BOT(build-operate-transfer)

The vehicle company established specially by the sponsors carries out the construction and operations of the project, which is usually a large turnkey project and installation of industries, for a limited period, and then the operational project is transferred to the relevant state authority, namely government agency turns over the operational project to the vehicle company. The vehicle companies in many developing countries are private ones. The BOT approach is likely to be a favorite to a government that is keen to minimize the impact on its capital budge, introduce increased efficiency from the private sector, and encourage foreign investment and introduction of new technology.

A BOT structure is normally based on a concession agreement between a government or a government agency, and the vehicle company established by the sponsors to carry out the construction and operation of the project. The liabilities undertaken by the project vehicle are substantial and the vehicle itself is incorporated specifically to obtain the concession. The sponsors might be required to providing independent commitments. Conversely, the sponsors will wish to ensure that the government party accepts that it might, in certain circumstances, need to be put into place and payments might need to be made for the benefits received from the project once it becomes operational.

Chapter 5 Commercial Banking

Sponsors are likely to require assurances as to a government intention on a range of further issues, which might affect the project while governments are unlikely to be either willing or able to fetter the future exercise of their legislative and administrative and administrative powers, sponsors might nevertheless try to ensure that adequate compensation shall be payable in the event that the government subsequently acts inconsistently with its expressed intentions and to the detriment of the project.

Government is concerned to ensure that proper work of maintenance and repair is carried out in order to provide an adequate service, to meet necessary safety and other requirements and to ensure that, on transfer at the end of the term, the government inherits an operational project and not simply a liability.

The Vehicle Company and sponsors are responsible for the finance of a BOT project. The risk of the finance is allocated between the parties(the vehicle company and the lender).The concession agreement is likely to affect substantially the project risk allocation and negotiations between the relevant parties on these issues should take account of the likely response of lenders to this allocation of risk. In BOT projects the host government not only plays a much greater role than in other projects, but also might have direct contact with the lender. Since the interests of the host government and the lenders will not necessarily coincide, it is essential for the sponsors and their advisers fully to appreciate the particular requirements of all parties involved.

参考译文

第Ⅱ部分　金融机构及其运作

第5章　商 业 银 行

5.1　中间业务

商业银行在金融活动中所发挥的主要功能如下所述。

(1)　通过银行信贷与投资业务来创造信用，创造货币。

(2)　吸收各类存款。

(3)　为各工商业企业提供支付和解款的运行机制。商业银行所能提供的中间业务包括：国际结算、信托业务、租赁业务和保理业务。

5.1.1　商业银行与客户之间的关系

1. 债务人-债权人关系

此关系建立在这样的基础上：商业银行从资金暂时盈余的客户处吸收了各种存款，银行只是暂时获得了资金的使用权，资金必在将来的某一特定时间归还给客户，因此银行在这样的金融活动中处于债务人地位，而存款客户则是债权人。

至于商业银行的中间业务，它就和前面所提的商业银行吸收存款、发放贷款活动大不一样，中间业务中的银行和客户之间不是一种债权-债务关系，而是一种委托-代理关系，即银行为中间业务的客户提供了一种代理服务。

2. 委托-代理关系

当银行不是直接和自己客户进行业务活动，而是有第三方参与双方之间的金融活动时，银行与客户之间的关系也将由债权—债务关系转变成一种委托-代理关系。

双方协定：当代理人同意担当委托人的代理人，代表其利益时，代理方就有权利依照代理合同的约定为委托方行使一定合法权益。

委托人的义务：

(1) 依照双方合同约定向代理人提供报酬。

(2) 偿还代理人的合理开支。

(3) 承担代理人代表其利益所进行的合法行为而产生的相应的负债与损失。

(4) 及时向代理人提供有关风险变化的信息。

代理人的义务：

(1) 遵守双方约定站在委托人的利益角度来为委托人争取最大利益。

(2) 谨慎和高效地贯彻执行委托人的指示和要求。

(3) 及时向委托人进行汇报。

(4) 对由于自己的不当行为导致的委托人的损失要向委托人进行赔偿。

(5) 向委托人提供及时可靠的信息。

5.1.2 中间业务的内容

1. 结算

结算业务为双方或超过两个的当事人之间资金结算和账户往来提供了一个公平合理的结账方式。

结算业务的发展经历了三个阶段：现金支付方式、信汇支付方式和电汇方式。同样，像汇票、支票和本票等结算工具也是国际结算中广泛使用的一种结算工具。它们也都代表了一种支付现金的权利，这种权利实际上是一种承诺，而不是某种具体形式的财产，因此也被归纳为一种结算工具。

2. 信托业务

个人与公司在其日常生产经营活动中往往需要一个值得信赖的外部组织或机构来帮助它们合理有效地管理自己的资产。商业银行为了满足这些客户的需要提供了信托业务。

信托业务：信托业务是一种当事人之间的信托关系。在信托业务中，受托人接受了财产所有人的委托为其管理和运用他的财产，从而为财产所有人获取收益。在一个正常的信托业务活动中通常有三方当事人：信托资产委托人(财产所有权人)、受益人和托管人(保管人)。

3. 租赁业务

租赁业务是出租人和承租人之间的一项合同行为，在该合同中：承租人获得了某一固定时期出租人的土地、地产、建筑、房屋、办公楼、机器设备或其他类型的动产的使用权。在这个租赁期内，租赁资产的所有权和使用权暂时由财产所有人(出租人)转移到使用人(承租人)手中，当合约期满，租赁资产的权利将会回复到所有人手中。

4. 保理业务

保理业务是通过将自己的应收账款进行无追索权的转让给第三方从而获得短期资金融通的一个有效方式。

5.2 国际结算

5.2.1 汇款

汇款是指不同国家的当事人之间通过银行进行资金划拨的一种方式。在这种结算方式中，国内银行根据自己客户的要求，将某笔资金由国内汇往自己在国外的分支机构或者是国外的代理银行，并通过它们最终将资金支付给该国的某个指定的个人或公司、组织、法人团体等。

1. 汇款方式或工具

国际汇款可以采用信汇、票汇和电汇等几种结算方式。但这几种方式都具有各自的特征，我们在稍后的章节中再作讨论。

2. 信汇(M/T)

信汇是指银行根据客户的要求，通过付款委托书、邮寄通知或汇出行开出的借项通知单等方式来进行资金划拨。无论是付款委托书、邮寄通知还是汇出行开出的借项通知单都必须通过查验汇出行相关当事人的签字或密码等方式加以确认。它将通知解付银行向受益人支付一笔特定数量的资金。解付行将会检查付款委托书收据上的相关当事人的签字来加以确认，一旦确认无误，将会由解付行通知受益人并向其支付，然后解付行再向汇出行索取资金。在实际操作中，汇出行将会在解付行在自己的账户上进行记账。

3. 票汇(M/T)

当客户希望能够自己将资金直接汇给当事的受益人时，经常使用票汇这种方式。在采取这种结算方式时，汇出人首先会向汇出行(寄单行)发出开立汇票的书面请求。汇出行(寄单行)在接受了客户的请求后，将会对客户(汇出人)的账户进行记账处理，扣除相应的款项，然后开立出一张银行承兑汇票并将其附送至汇出人。这样汇出人就可以将汇票携带在身并在需要时向自己国外的收款人进行支付。收款人在接收到汇票以后，就可以向付款人所在银行出示票据请求付款，或者收款人也可以直接向自己的开户行来出售票据从而获取款项。付款人所在行在收到收款人出示的票据将会先对票据的签名进行鉴别，当发现汇票无问题后付款人所在行将会向收款人进行支付。付款人接下来将会通过自己和汇出行(寄单行)的代理协议来向汇出行索回自己支付的款项。

4. 电汇(T/T)

电汇是指通过全世界银行间金融电信协会来进行的支付。除了汇出行向解付行发出的指令是通过电报/电缆/SWIFT 方式传达,而不是通过信件的方式传达的以外，这种电汇方式与信汇几乎是完全一致的。因此，电汇比信汇更加便捷、迅速，但是也更加昂贵。当汇款的款项数额较大或者汇款时间限定比较紧张时，经常采用这种电汇方式。全球间的汇款大约有 90% 是通过电汇方式进行的。

5.2.2 跟单托收

1. 跟单托收的流程

跟单托收是指银行站在卖方的利益角度向卖方进行付款，而卖方将相关的结算单据转交给买方。

当出口方不愿意在一个未结算的往来账目基础上进行双边交易而又对原始记录的信用安全等级要求不高时，经常采用跟单托收。在跟单托收结算中，如果进口商没有进行付款或者未能承兑汇票时，进口商就不能获取货物，因此跟单托收比一般结算更加安全。相关的参与银行是没有付款职责和义务的。

在跟单托收中，当货物进行发运过程中，出口商不能确定此时进口商是否如实支付自己所欠的款项，因此这种结算方式在以下的情形中将会更加适用。

- 当出口商对进口商的付款意愿和能力没有任何质疑时。
- 当进口商所在国的政治、经济、法律环境是稳定的情形下。
- 当买方所在国对进口(外汇汇兑)没有任何限制或者买方所在国政府已经发放了一切必需的授权证书和特许权。

2. 跟单托收的步骤

跟单托收的整个流程从进、出口商之间建立买卖合同的第一步开始一直贯穿到整个交易流程的结束，因此它可能包括许多独立的步骤。但通常情况下，一个完整的跟单托收流程包括如下三个步骤。

步骤 1　制定交单条款

出口商在向进口商要价商谈合同时提出自己的支付条款，或者与进口商商谈双方达成一致，将此记录在双方的买卖合同中。

步骤 2　托收委托书以及相关文件的传达

在签订销售合同后，出口商直接将货物发送给买方。同时，出口商将准备好一切必需的相关单据(发票、提货单、保险凭证和货物原产地证明书等)，然后出口商将准备好的齐全的单据与托收委托书一并送交至自己的开户行(寄单行、汇出行)。寄单行(汇出行)在收到这些单据以后，将这些单据以及必需的指令一并传达至代收银行。

步骤 3　提示单据和结算

代收银行在收到了一切相关单据以后，将会通知进口商货物到达并传达关于货物提取的相关条款和要求。进口商及时支付款项或者承兑汇票，然后从代收行处收到货物单据。然后，代收行将收到的货款汇至托收行，由托收行将款项贷记至出口商的账户。

3. 跟单托收的参与者

在一个正常的跟单托收中通常有如下四方参与者：

- 出口商(卖方、收款人)。
- 托收行。
- 代收行，这里的代收行是指托收委托书中所涉及的任何一家银行，其职责是向进口商出示单据。
- 进口商(买方、付款人)。

4. 设定跟单托收的条款

当一个潜在的外国买主向出口商提出购买意向时，同时也会要求出口商给出自己的买卖要求和其他相关条款。

A. 付款交单(D/P)

付款交单是指提示行(代收行)只有在向付款人提示跟单汇票要求其付款而付款人及时付款以后才能够向其交单。在国际惯例中，即期支付是指不迟于货物到达。

B. 承兑交单(D/A)

在这种情况下，提示行(代收行)在付款人承兑远期汇票后，就可以将货运单据交给付款人，而付款人将会在 30～180 天内或者未来的某一固定日期进行付款。

5. 托收委托书

当采取托收委托形式时，有以下几点事项需要我们特别注意：买方地址，托收类型，单据，提示行(代收行)的名称和地址，汇票，委托书和费用，必须事项，特别备注，银行账户和签名。

6. 将单据传递至代收行

寄单行将单据与其他必需的指令一齐发至买方所在国的一家银行。

托收的费用比较低廉，对于客户来说也是物有所值。银行不仅可以自由支配自己的富有经验的专家，而且可以运用全球通信网的资源，因此这种方式可以保证及时在异常情况下支付、单据与信息都能安全可靠地被传达和转移。

5.2.3 跟单信用证

1. 原则与特征

信用证的出现为国际贸易结算提供了一种新的结算手段，从而在这种方式下出口商获得付款的安全性得以保证，而进口商也能够确保自己的货物与商业贸易契约中的相一致并获得了妥善处理，因而进口商也就能够安心支付款项。

《跟单信用证统一惯例》提供了一些基本原则：跟单信用证的独立性以及跟单信用证只处理单据，而和货物无关。

2. 跟单信用证的运作

根据 UCP 条例的规定，银行只对单据进行审核，只要受益人提交了符合信用证条款的单据，开证行就必须付款，并不受货物合同的约束。

这也就意味着银行必须加倍小心地对单据进行审核，对于提交的单据与信用证条款或者各个单据之间任何不一致或矛盾的地方都必须指出。

信用证首先是银行同业之间的一项业务，通知行或保兑行是在开证行开立的不可撤销或者无条件付款承诺的信用证的前提下操作业务。这里需要开证行具有较高的专业水平。当然开证行对通知行或承兑行也有同样的期待。否则开证行将会选择别的银行来进行自己的信用证业务。

开证行开立了信用证以后就要承担开证申请人的信用风险。一旦开立了信用证，它就对开证申请人的信用以及商品价格的变化不关心了，因为这个承诺将是独立的也是最终的。

就像前面所说的，当信用证与单据出现细微不一致时，拒付往往就会产生。而挑剔单证不一致的原因往往是进口商希望在支付之前就占有货物或者收到货物后发现货物与合同不一致。

当然信用证对单据的内容要求越细致，单证不一致的现象也就越有可能发生。因此银行的专业人员应该从专业角度出发适当地提醒他的客户稍加注意，选择合适的单据和合适的描述单据的条款。

银行业务人员细致谨慎地审核单据，不仅是为了保护自己客户的利益，也是为自己在信用证业务中的合作银行考虑。通过仔细审核单据，提醒开证行对不一致处的注意，通知行/保兑行可以有效地阻止开证行因为误导而进行的支付行为。实际上，如果开证行在后来收到了不一致的单据，而事先又未能得到提醒时，开证行或者债权人可能无法追回已经支付的款项。这也就意味着买方将来可能不会有任何的追索权。

最后，如果任一银行发现了任何可能存在的损害各参与方的舞弊或欺诈行为时，该银行都必须及时通知信用证项下的自己的合作银行。

当出现单证不一致的情况时，开证行必须在一个合理时间内及时地通知寄单行。在新的 UCP 条例中，要求在 7 个工作日内。换句话说，开证行必须将最近发现的单据不符点在 7 个工作日内通知寄单行，开证行将通知寄单行由其来处理相关单据并等待进一步的指示。另一个值得牢记的就是所有的不一致的地方必须是同一时间向相关行提醒，发现某一个附加的不一致处而在稍后单独传达是不可接受的，也是不允许的。

3. 信用证中的欺诈行为

信用证的独立性和"单证一致"这两个特征都是可能在实践中产生欺诈行为的地方。在信用证结算项下，出口商只要将符合信用证条款的单据交给出口地银行就可以获得货款，而开证行只要通知行提供相符的单据就将对其进行偿付，开证行对于信用证中具体的契约的运行情况毫不关心。因此一些欺诈行为就会乘机而入，从而给正当营业的商人和银行带来潜在的损失。不法分子可以将信用证作为他们轻易谋取非法利益的一个工具。

金融专业英语

- 制造虚假单据。
- 伪造跟单信用证。
- 信用证汇票金额巨大。

在任何一种体系下都有可能发生诈骗和洗钱的犯罪行为，它们还会出现在信用证和备用信用证的业务中。

伪造的单据隐藏于跟单信用证中，虽然比较少见但是不易被人发觉。在这方面的犯罪分子往往都是技能高超的专家，因而也就能够完美地伪造出看似真实的单据。银行的专业熟练的工作人员及其对基本单据的反复核对和校验，这些违法的欺诈行为绝大部分都能被发现。当一个不熟悉的受益人提供了完美的信用证项下的单据并要求银行立即进行大额款项支付时，银行更应加以谨慎处理。

伪造的跟单信用证相对来说比较容易发现。曾经一段时间，伪造的跟单信用证通常看起来都是由非洲国家的银行开出的，而现在此类信用证越来越多看似来自东欧国家银行，或者是根本不存在的国家。它们大都看起来是原始的，但是通过银行人员对细节仔细反复地核对往往都能被查出。

当受益人从开证行处直接收到跟单信用证而不是由受益人本地的银行通知其时，这时对信用证的真伪性就应该产生疑问。受益人在发货或者开始合同行为之前应该先就信用证的权威性向自己的银行进行咨询。他当然也不应该签署保证书。

这种技术通常也会被用来以所谓的高效投资来吸引受害人，这些受害人一旦上当，他们的资金就会因为无法得到任何的偿付而损失。同时，这种类型的信用证也会被用作进行金钱欺诈。

欺诈人往往会在信用证中采用一些国际一流银行的名称来吸引更多的受害人或银行上当。

5.2.4　保函

1. 担保的类型

当买方要求卖方提供担保来保证买方自己的权益时，银行就会应出口方的申请向进口方开立书面保证文件。卖方通常会采取以下几种常见形式的保函。

(1) 投标保函或者投标保证书

当卖方对某项合同进行投标时，卖方往往会被要求提供一定的投保保证金，通常保证金数额是卖方开价的 2%~5%之间。投保保证书的目的是为了保证将来投标人已经改变了他投标的条款和内容或者在投标期撤回自己的投标时，甚至在他中标后却不在合约上签字时，受益人的付款不受影响。

(2) 履约保函

这是最常使用的保证类型，而且当其他类型的保证都不是必需的时，此保证也会被要求提供。

履约保证通常会承诺支付合同金额的 5%~10%的款项，当买方宣称卖方并没有完全履行合约时，这往往会发生作用。当卖方为了获得合同而提供了投保保证书以后，如果投标成功了，这时投标保证书通常会被履约保证书取代。如果该合同里规定某些义务的履行需要担保，比如交货、质量担保和安装等，这时履约担保就相应起到担保履行这些义务的作用。

(3) 预付款保函

在贸易合同签订中为了满足卖方的要求或者弥补一些最初的费用支出，这时就会采取预付款保证。当合同中交货的行为未能完成时，这种预付款保证就可以用来保证偿还款项的安全性。预付款保证的数量通常是合同价格总额的 10%~20%之间。另外，当该保证可以以书面形式约定，只有在卖方收到经双方协定的预付款时才有效时，这个预付款保证就更为可取。当交货货物数量比银行所提示单据中的货运单据中的数量有一定比例的减少时，这种预付款保证也是经常采用的。另一种可以表示的减少是所完成的工作与银行所提示的实际完成证明书之间的差异。对于保证事项中债务减少的变化程度必须非常明确地指出，这也是保证书中十分重要的内容。

(4) 尾款保函

有一些合同中会约定在买方确定所有程序都已经完成并且接收了货物之前，不能全部支付款项，而是预留最高至总款项的 10%的金额作为尾款保证金，以保证未来卖方能够得到支付。这种保证既保证了卖方的权利义务的一致性，也是买方能够在保险期结束前得到预留款的保证。

(5) 维修保函

在建筑合同或其相关合同中，通常会要求有维修保证。这个条款确保了设计者在维修期内都能保证完成自己的义务，以保证最终整项工程可以完成。在维修周期中，维修保证也可以用来取代预留款。

2. 见索即付银行保函

银行保函是银行以自身信誉为承担风险的一方提供保障的一种结算方式。银行保函是银行根据申请人的请求，向受益人开立的书面承诺，保证在受益人提交书面请求和符合保函中所规定的单据时，赔付一定的金额。在出现问题时，银行往往需要从卖方获得赔偿。

保函往往需要提供一系列的独立的单据，比如仲裁裁决证明书或运货代理商的货运单据复印件，因此银行保函也被称为有条件的保函。

保函虽然源于一定的商业合约，但一经出具，其本身的效力却不依附于基础合同而独立存在，其基础合同的消亡并不意味着保函也随之自动失效。尤其是"见票即付"条款的规定使得这一特点更加突出。

进口商往往也会在商品买卖合同中加入一定的条款，从而及时有效地防止担保人的错误担保行为。具体来说，是将有问题的单证及时迅速地呈递给担保人，从而防止其做出不恰当的担保。公共机构的证明书、独立专家的意见、进出口双方共同签署的声明、仲裁裁决书或者类似的文件都是可以接受的。这些文件的相关细节应该尽可能多地在跟单信用证中出现，这是非常重要的，这样我们就可以从中得到贸易合同的更多的参考信息。

保函的自身特征就是要求受益人必须在要求付款时提供保函中明确规定的独立单据，因此保函相对来说不易存在风险。

3. 直接担保

直接担保是出口方的银行在信用证下根据申请人的申请向国外受益人开立保函，以承担担保责任的一种方式。担保保证人必将会完成自己的职责。而受益人也必须由自己所在的银行来进行担保保证自己的主张签名的正确性。

4. 间接担保

间接担保是申请人请求当地银行以提供反担保的形式委托受益人所在地的银行代其开立保函，并代其承担赔付责任的保函开立方式。一般来说，在外资银行申明其受益人提出了该担保款项的支付要求时，该担保行就要履行其付款义务。

自然，当外国银行参与到保函业务中时，间接担保比直接担保更容易产生问题。外国银行的保函又会受所在国的法律的限制，因而由此产生的一系列问题，通知行及其客户是必须承担的。

5.2.5 备用信用证

备用信用证又称担保信用证，是指不以清偿商品交易的价款为目的，而以贷款融资或担保债务偿还为目的所开立的信用证。由于这种信用证仅在申请人不能偿还借款或不能履约时，由开证行对受益人进行赔偿，如已还款或已履约就不需支付了，因此它是备用性质的信用证。备用信用证是由银行应申请人的请求或以自身名义，向受益人出具的，保证凭规定的单据向受益人支付一定数额款项的书面凭证。

备用信用证包括以下类型。

(1) 履约担保。在工程项目中，投标人中标后就是承包人，应与工程业主签订合同，并向业主提供履约的银行担保，即备用信用证，以保证承包人如不履行合同规定的责任和义务，开证行就按信用证金额偿付受益人因此而受到的损失。

(2) 按揭条件违约保证。这种信用证是银行承诺当借款人不能按期偿还公司票据、州或地方政府债券时，将由银行来进行偿还。这种信用证使得借款人以更低的成本或更灵活的方式来融资。银行为了成功地向客户提供这种信用担保，它必须保证自己的信用等级要高于自己的担保客户。这些年来，美国的许多银行的信用等级都已经降低了，因此有越来越多它们的竞争对手(包括国外的银行和保险公司)已经在信用担保市场占领了更大的份额。

备用信用证中开证行的清偿款项的责任是可能发生的。因为备用信用证承诺了当客户不能对第三方履行合约或者不能偿还款项时，银行将进行承担，银行为申请人提供了信用担保，因此银行开立备用信用证时也要向申请人收取一定的费用。银行开立备用信用证的主要优势有如下几点。

(1) 信用证使得开征银行因为提供了担保服务而获取相当于信用证金额的 0.5%～1%比例的收入。

(2) 信用证开立使得银行在不需占用自己资源的情况下为客户提供成本更加低廉的融资业务。

(3) 信用证的成本通常也会比较低廉，因为开证行通常在向客户提供担保服务时，银行可以通过该客户最近一次的信贷从而获取该客户的金融财务状况，因此节约了调查成本。

(4) 通常来说备用信用证项下开证行的付款责任发生的可能性是比较低的。

5.3 信用贷款

5.3.1 商业信贷

从贷款期限来划分，贷款可以分为两种类型。贷款期限在 1 年或 1 年以内的称为短期信贷，而贷款期限在 1 年以上的称为中长期贷款。短期贷款通常是用来满足日常营运成本之需，而长期贷款通常是用来对固定资产进行投资。当然贷款也可以根据贷款的目的或者贷款合约安排的性质来进行划分。

5.3.2 专项贷款

1. 出口信贷

出口信贷是政府(政府信贷机构)为了支持出口企业从而通过商业银行

向相关贸易商从事的信用服务。它又可以分为买方信贷和卖方信贷。

在买方信贷中，出口方银行向进口商(进口商银行担保机构)或者进口商银行来提供贷款，进口商获得贷款融资以满足其购买出口方货物的需求。买方信贷通常包括以下内容和条件。

- 贷款通常是用来满足从发放贷款的国家购买资本货物及其相关服务的要求。
- 贷款金额通常是合乎规定的商业合约价值的 85%，而剩余款项的支付必须是以现金形式或其他商业贷款形式进行。
- 各项已获得融资的信贷款项的期限通常是不同的，一般在 5～10 年间。
- 贷款款项的下达应该遵循这样的原则，即每半年分批发放，开始的时间由出口信贷机构或贸易合同决定。
- 贷款利率通常要与市场上的利率或经合组织的规定以及短期国库券的利率相一致。
- 承诺费是从借款合同签订之时起算到贷款款项支付为止，按照年来计算。
- 管理费则是按照贷款数额来进行计算。
- 由代理机构决定的信贷保险费用可以通过借款来进行支付，也可以加入到供货合同中商品的价值中去，从而获得出口信贷融资。

买方信贷将会依照进口方银行是否直接提供信贷担保而采取不同的程序。当进口方银行提供担保时，其流程如下。

- 进出口双方银行共同商定一个总的出口信贷的框架。进口方银行提出要求，然后出口方银行来做出是否同意，并制定具体的合同内容。
- 进出口方签订商品合同。
- 进出口方各自独立地向进口方银行和出口方银行提出申请。
- 出口方银行与进口方银行签订一个独立的贷款合同以对出口信用评级机构进行融资，当出口信用评级机构同意后，出口信贷合同就正式生效。

在第二种情况下，将采取如下流程。

- 进出口方签订商品合同。
- 出口方和进口方各自向出口方银行和进口方银行提出申请。
- 出口方银行与进口方签订借款合同，而进口方银行在进出口银行双方都同意此贷款以后向出口方银行开立担保。
- 出口方银行就信贷合同向出口方信贷评级机构提出评级申请，在评级机构批准后出口信贷合同就正式生效。

另一种形式的出口信贷是卖方信贷方式。在卖方信贷中，出口方银行向出口方提供贷款，从而出口商在贸易合同中添加了特定条款，允许进口方可以每半年支付一次货款，因此卖方信贷中进口方支付货款的时间延长，而出口方从银行处提前获得了货款资金，可以看作银行提供的中长期信贷。在这种方式下，汇票的发行者是出口商，但必须征得买方的同意。卖方信贷通常的条款内容和条件要求都是与买方信贷一致的。卖方信贷的具体流程如下。

- 出口方与进口方就商品合同或者服务合同进行商谈并最终确定。通常合同中的支付货款条款要求进口商进行分期付款。
- 出口方和进口方各自向出口方银行和进口方银行提出申请。进口方银行向出口方开立保函。出口方银行与出口方签订贷款合同。在信贷评级机构进行评级后贷款合同和商品贸易合同开始正式生效。

2. 福费廷

福费廷是银行从出口商手中无追索权地购买各种票据(包括汇票、本票等多种票据)。事实上，卖方所在国的银行(卖方银行、供应方银行或者出口方银行)往往采取一定的折扣来购买汇票以此弥补将来买方银行(或称买方所在国的银行)向其请求追索权(而出口方银行已无法再向出口商行使该权)的损失。福费廷主要用于对出口商货物出口的中短期融资。福费廷一词源自法语中的"forfait"一词，其含义是放弃权利(福费廷中即指放弃追索权)。

福费廷的基本特征如下。首先，买方先预付合同价款的 15%～20%。

剩余金额则可以通过福费廷市场得到满足。在福费廷项下，卖方获得的安全保障与其可能从保兑信用证中获得的是一样的，因为卖方银行同样承诺了只要出口方提供合适的票据就会向其进行无追索的支付。

在见票即付或者其他短期信贷中，跟单信用证是经常被采用的。而福费廷通常用于提供大型机器设备买卖中的融资，其期限通常是中期的。

福费廷银行通常要求经国际知名银行担保的授权书，这样可以减低风险，也可以使得福费廷银行能够比较容易地在二级市场将票据卖出。

福费廷只能采取几种有限的货币进行交易。通常采用的货币是美元、欧元和瑞士法郎，这同样可以大大降低银行的汇兑风险。

福费廷成本的高低通常会受以下因素的影响：所采用的货币的利率水平、进口国的信贷风险评估等级的高低和银行所提供的担保水平等。

贴现银行从事该业务所关心的即是否能从中赢利。这通常也取决于欧洲市场的资金成本高低。贴现银行还要收取与担保银行有关的政治风险和转移风险的费用。

目前存在一个规模较小的、只对一些专业福费廷商人开放的二级福费廷交易市场。这个市场风险较高，因此投资者会要求拥有资金追索权。但是这个市场的回报率要比其他类型的等金额投资高。

福费廷的工作流程如下。

- 卖方开出以买方为付款人的汇票，到期时进行承兑。或者买方开出以卖方为收款人的本票。这两种票据的到期期限要和买方的信贷期限一致。在绝大多数情况下，付款是在信贷期内分期进行的。然后会开出一套具有相应到期期限的汇票或本票。

- 票据经买方银行担保后，传递给卖方。出口商通过向本国的福费廷银行贴现卖出自己的票据从而获取现金支付，而不必等到票据到期。出口商在福费廷项下将会无追索权地将票据背书转让给银行。而福费廷银行会因为这个票据已经经由进口方银行担保，因而很乐意进行此项业务。而贴现率也在一定程度上弥补了无追索权可能带来的损失。在极个别的情况下，福费廷银行可能没有获得进口方银行的担保。这很可能是因为，票据中涉及的进口国信用风险极低，因而应该不会发生支付问题。

- 在商品合同最终敲定之前，对于买卖双方来说，都应该明确各自的银行是愿意参与合作的，这是非常重要的。出口商向银行发出要约，要求其提出其贴现的报价。大部分银行都比较愿意提前 1 年到 18 个月来购买未到期票据。出口商还必须承担承诺费。

- 当银行买入出口商手中未到期的票据时，银行支付给出口商的款项通常会比其从进口商处获得现金支付的款项要少。作为选择，出口方也可以在开立汇票时以低于合同金额的数额开立，以此来承担部分的贷款融资成本，并促成合同更加容易地完成。

- 福费廷银行在票据到期时向进口商提出支付。进口商将会向福费廷银行进行全额支付，这个款项是整个贸易合同金额加上信用证项下进口商应承担的其他费用。最终结果，就像类似于买方从福费廷银行以一定的利率获得贷款融资。

福费廷案例

如果你的客户(一家年营业额近 1500 万瑞士法郎的出口公司)正在试图与 XYZ 国的一家国有企业签订一项关于供应纺织机器设备的交易合同。该商品合同的总价值为 500 万瑞士法郎，交货期限最高为 24 个月。招标文件指出，该设备的出口必须以融资方式提供。通过与非洲经济委员会的初步调查研究显示，这项交易的融资比率为 95%。

你的客户对于传统的出口信贷服务(即愿意分担非经委会的风险)感兴趣，并提交了相关的融资申请表。

问题:

(1) 你是否会提供出口信贷支持?

(2) 你的信贷协议考虑哪些方面的内容?

(3) 此出口信贷的总额是多少?

答案:

(1) 出口信贷在原则上是可行的。

(2) 调查/确认/需要考虑的事项

> a. 是否贷款能够促使其在交付期限内履行自己的合同义务？
>
> b. 出口商是否有能力来履行金额如此之大的合同？
>
> - 过去的出口记录如何？
> - 出口贸易额或营业额是多少？
> - 主要出口的国家有哪些？
> - 是否依赖于上游供应商？
> - 是设计加工的产品还是标准的产成品？
> - 与 XYZ 国合作的经历如何？
>
> c. 该出口商在你的银行是否对以下项有信贷额度的限制？
>
> - 投标担保
> - 预付订金保证
> - 履约担保
> - 必需的出口前的金融支持
> - 对非经委组织所承担风险的追索
>
> d. 是否有即期付款或预付款的信用证？
>
> - 通过你的银行开立(交叉销售的可能)。
> - 信用证是否由你的银行承兑？(你对信用证开出行是否有什么限制？)
>
> (3) 425 万瑞士法郎。

5.3.3 银团贷款

1. 银团贷款定义

银团贷款是指由一家银行牵头，多家银行共同参与为某一个企业提供贷款的信用贷款组织形式。参与银团贷款的多家银行共同分享贷款收益，共同承担贷款风险。

银团贷款通常一开始是由一家银行和一个企业签订贷款协议，但由于这项贷款金额巨大，通常超过 1000 万美元，银行出于分散风险和控制风险的考虑，往往会考虑将这笔贷款转贷出去，由几家大银行共同承担贷款，从而降低风险损失。这时，牵头银行往往是在多家竞争银行中最终胜出的银行，因而也就承担了相对较大比例的贷款，同时也要承担起组织其余多家银行共同参与贷款的义务。最终这项贷款协议将会由一个独立的贷款企业和多家参与的银行共同签订。

随着企业单笔信贷资金的急剧增长，单一的贷方银行往往无法满足企业的需求，因此，银团贷款最近几年发展十分迅猛。由于银团贷款数额少则千万，高则数十亿美元，很多银行出于法律限制或者风险暴露与补偿的考虑，通常都不愿意或者不能够满足此类客户的需求。同时，很多银行也会考虑到未来对同样客户继续发放长期贷款融资的空间，从而有可能影响到当前的企业需求。

在每一个银团贷款中，都会安排一家代理银行，由它来负责此贷款从签署协议一直到后来的贷款归还的整个过程。考虑到代理银行工作职责的复杂性，通常都会由借款人向代理行支付一笔费用。这笔费用与其他支付给银行的费用是完全独立、无关联的。代理行的具体职责如下：贷款利率的确定、贷款资金的划拨、确保借款人能够及时归还利息和本金以及其他贷款协议项下的各项义务。

2. 银团贷款的目的

银团贷款主要用于以下情况的融资：大型发展计划、规模较大的工程项目、资金周转的暂时性的不平衡、大型资本项目投资、成本超支的项目、公司兼并与并购、公司长短期债务的重组及公司长期债务的合理再融资。

绝大部分银团贷款企业要能在银团贷款中获得成功，必须妥善地完成以下四项基本功能：信息备忘录的准备、相关文件资料的整理、联合贷款功能和代理功能。

信息备忘录将会传递至各个潜在的参与银行处，上面记载借款人的详细信息，包括借款人过去的信用记录、借款人未来状况的预测、借款人的基本管理状况以及对借款人所在国经济前景的分析。

牵头银行通常要承担防止信用欺诈或者疏于职守的义务和职责。同时必须强调的是，借款人必须保证自己的信息都是精确完整的，以及确保任何独立的验证或签字都不是由管理者自身给出的。牵头银行在当地或国际法律组织的协助之下，能够及时准备好一份可行的贷款协议以及其他必需的文件。所有文件的编制都必须适应与满足银团贷款中各参与者的要求。

为了使银团贷款能够正常有序地进行下去，牵头银行在满足了借款人的各种特别需求以后，牵头银行必须将款项发放到一个国际金融组织机构的户头上。这是银团贷款的固有特征。深入了解了市场以及借款人的相关信息后，银团贷款的牵头银行就可以确保在当前的情况下，考虑了各种竞争因素以后，自己所发放的贷款是确实可行的。

作为一个代理机构，牵头银行将会在整个贷款期间内对贷款进程进行监督与管理，同时他也将作为借款人以及其他参与银行的咨询人和建议者，向他们提供关于贷款的先决条件要求、贷款的特征与贷款担保方面的内容。

5.3.4 BOT(建设-经营-转移)

由发起人专门成立的一家运营公司通常要负责一个大型工程项目的各项运营与预算。这种大型项目可能是一个大型工程承包项目或者工程安装项目，在经营一段时期以后，该项目就会转交给有关当局，通常是由政府机构转交给某个专门公司。在大部分发展中国家中，这个专门公司通常都是私营的。采用 BOT 方式以后，政府可以克服其公共预算不足的困难，引入私人部门的经营高效率机制，吸引大量外国资金以及积极吸纳各种新技术。

正常的 BOT 是建立在政府或政府机构与某一特定运营公司之间的特许协议基础之上的。由项目中介公司所承担的该项目的债务是巨大的，责任是具体的，而且这个特许运营商将来会成立一家专门的公司以获得特许经营权。发起人可能会被要求独立承担义务。相反，发起人也会希望通过这种方式使政府确保该项目将会有序进行，同时在项目投产运行一定时间以后，发起人能够从中获取收益。

发起人希望能够获得政府的保证，从而保证项目的实施不会受到太多政府行为的限制。同时发起人希望当政府后来的行为与他们一开始拟定的目标产生偏差从而导致项目进展受损时，发起人能够获得一定程度的补偿。

政府则更加关心保养与维修工作是否得到了保证，从而确保将来能够提供足够的服务，满足必要的安全性；同时希望确保接下来在为了合同的一定时期到来开始进行实际转交时，政府能够获得运营良好的项目而不仅仅是一种债务。

无论是运营的公司还是政府，都必须筹集 BOT 项目的资金。因此，项目的资金风险也就是由合作双方共同承担的。特许协议对于参与到 BOT 项目中的各方的风险分担和具体内容安排都会有较大的影响。在 BOT 项目中，政府在此项目中发挥的作用往往是要显著于在政府在其他项目中的作用，同时政府也与贷方签订了直接的协议，建立了直接联系。由于政府和贷方的利益并不总是必然的一致，因此，对于发起人来说尽可能满足各方的各种特殊需求和要求就显得至关重要了。

5.3.4 BOT(建设-经营-转让)

Chapter 5　Commercial Banking

Subject Topic(命题对话)

The Growth of the National Economy

(国民经济的增长)

A: Why is it necessary to achieve the 8% GDP growth rate in 2009?

B: I think the first reason to achieve the 8% growth rate is to provide a strong material support to deepen the economic reform and to enhance the ability to deal with complicated situations. The second reason is to alleviate the pressure of unemployment in society.

A: I guess it is also to increase financial revenue.

B: The 21st century is of knowledge economy. Countries will intensify their competition in high technology. We could increase investment in advanced technology if we had a sound base of financial revenue at the same time. Increased revenue will also strengthen the resistance to financial risks with a sound economic base and improve people's living standards.

A: What kind of measures should the central government take to achieve the 8% GDP growth in 2009?

B: I think the government will stimulate the domestic demand with effective monetary policies.

A: What is the relationship between domestic demand and GDP growth?

B: As we know, effective domestic demand and international demand are two main driving forces for economic growth. However, under the influence of the global financial crisis, China's export competitiveness is somewhat weakened and that leaves domestic demand to pull economic growth. Therefore, on one hand, efforts should be made to reduce interest rates and expand credit scale to promote investment in the economic sectors such as agriculture, infrastructure construction and technology innovation to

127

 金融专业英语

guarantee economic growth. In this year the government will formulate more active financial support to augment its investment in key economic sectors.

Questions and Answers(专业问答)

1. What are the payment methods commonly used by banks?
    —They are mail transfer, telegraphic transfer and demand draft.
2. Please point out the basic party of credit business.
    —They are:

    a. the applicant

    b. the beneficiary

    c. issuing bank

    d. advising bank/negotiating bank/confirming bank
3. What are the major risks that banks often experience? Please list at least five kinds of them.
    —They are :

    a. credit risk/market risk

    b. interest rate risk

    c. exchange rate risk

    d. political risk

    e. price risk
    f. internal risk/management risk
    g. liquidity risk
4. What are the principles of commercial bank management?
    —They are :
    a. liquidity
    b. safety
    c. profitability

Chapter 5   Commercial Banking

5. During the management of banks, what are the basic requirements of
    liquidity policy?

    —They are :

        a. assets hold by a bank can be encashed without depreciation or
           used to pay outside liabilities in any time

        b. a bank has absolute certainty to obtain required current funds at a
           relatively low cost in any time

6. Western countries usually use 5C loan credit appraisal method. What
    is 5C?

    —It's character, capacity, capital, collateral and conditions.

Exercises(练习)

Reading Comprehension

Passage One

For a great variety of reasons, individuals or corporations may desire a
reliable outside entity to administer their assets. To meet this need, and to attract
large depositors, banks offer trust services. As wealth in China has increased,
the need for trust services has grown. Management of trusts involves both
investing the funds for growth and carrying out specific instructions regarding
them.

To better understand the trust services banks offer, we should first
understand what trust is. Legally speaking, trust is a fiduciary relationship in
which one person is trusted by the holder of the legal title to property, subject to
an equitable obligation to keep or use the property for the benefit of the holder
or a designated party.

In early times trusts had their purpose for the preservation of property in
order that favored individuals or institutions might benefit from the income from

129

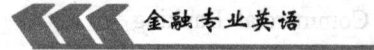

the principal of the trusts or come into the possession of the principal itself. In the establishment of a trust, there are primarily three principal parties involved:

- The trustor, or party who creates the trust, who is also known as the settler, grantor, or

- The beneficiary, an individual or charitable organization, for whose benefit the fund is established. A beneficiary may have a interest in trust income, corpus or both; and a present interest, commencing with the trust's creation, or a future interest, commencing when a specified event occurs, or both; and

- The trustee, who is charged with the arrangement and preservation of the property that constitutes the trust estate. It can also be one or more individuals, or an organization (e.g. a bank) who holds legal title to property placed in trust and is responsible for administering the property for benefit of the trust beneficiary or beneficiaries.

Among the various types of trusts in terms of provisions affecting distribution to the beneficiaries are the following:

Trust Deposits are deposits that are made by one person as trustee for the other person. Such the deposits are made under trustee account agreements executed in advance and subject to the terms and conditions of the agreements. Despite the usual provisions in such agreements for discharging of the bank for withdrawals by the trustee, which has both a personal account and a trustee account in the bank, the bank might become subject to constructive notice and inquiry in cases of loss to beneficiaries through steady and large withdrawals from the trustee account to personal account.

1. In the establishment of a trust, there are primarily_____.

    A. three principal parties involved: trustor, trustee, and grantor

    B. three principal parties involved: settler, trustee, and grantor

    C. three principal parties involved: trustor, donor, and grantor

    D. three principal parties involved: settler, trustee, and beneficiary

Chapter 5 Commercial Banking

2. The party who creates the trust is_____.
    A. the trustee   B. the beneficiary
    C. trustor   D. none of the above is correct
3. None of the following statements is true except_____.
    A. the trustor is responsible for administering the property for the
       benefit of the trustee only
    B. the trustee is responsible for administering the property for the
       benefit of the trustor only
    C. the trustee is responsible for administering the property for the
       benefit of the beneficiary or beneficiaries
    D. the trustor is responsible for administering the property for the
       benefit of the trustee or a designated party
4. Trust Deposits are made under trustee account agreements_____.
    A. signed in advance   B. fulfilled in advance
    C. drafted in advance   D. signed and fulfilled in advance
5. For withdrawals by the trustee where a trustee has both a personal
    account and a trustee account in the bank, _____.
    A. the bank is not subject to inquiry in cases of loss to beneficiaries
       through steady and large withdrawals from the trustee account to
       personal account
    B. the bank is always subject to inquiry in cases of loss to beneficiaries
       through steady and large withdrawals from the trustee account to
       personal account
    C. the bank might become subject to inquiry in cases of loss to beneficiaries
       through steady and large withdrawals from the trustee account to
       personal account
    D. the trustor might become subject to inquiry in cases of loss to
       beneficiaries through steady and large withdrawals from the trustee
       account to personal account

131

Passage two

Types of documentary credit include: payment credit, acceptance credit, and deferred payment credit, etc..

Payment Credit. The meaning of the term "payment" is self-evident. The nominated bank will pay the beneficiary on receipt of the specified documents and on fulfillment of all the terms of credit.

Sometimes the issuing bank nominates itself as paying bank, in which case payment will be made on receipt of the correct documents at their counters abroad. On other occasions, usually with confirmed credit, the issuing bank will nominate the advising bank to pay.

The term "payment" only applies to sight drafts, and sometimes, fixed time drafts (deferred payment).

Negotiation Credit. Sometimes the issuing bank will nominated the advising bank to negotiate a credit, or it may even make the credit freely negotiable, in which case any bank is a nominated bank.

If a bank negotiates a credit, it will advance money to the beneficiary on presentation of the required documents and will charge interest on the advance from the date of the advance until such time as it receives reimbursement from the issuing bank.

Such negotiation advances are said to be with recourse, so that if payment is not ultimately forthcoming from the issuing bank, the negotiating bank will be able to claim repayment from the beneficiary of the advance, plus interest. If the negotiating bank has confirmed the credit, the advance will be on a "without recourse" basis, provided the terms of the credit have been complied with.

1.   Under payment credit, the nominated bank_____.

    A. will pay the beneficiary unconditionally

    B. will pay the beneficiary after checking that the received documents meet the credit requirements

    C. remit the funds to the beneficiary only on receipt of the time draft

Chapter 5　Commercial Banking

　　　D. is nominated by any bank

2. Under negotiation credit, the credit＿＿＿＿.

　　　A. is always negotiated through the advising bank

　　　B. is sometimes negotiated through the advising bank

　　　C. can always be negotiated through any bank

　　　D. None of the above is true.

3. If a bank negotiates a credit, it will＿＿＿＿.

　　　A. advance money to the beneficiary without charging any interest

　　　B. advance money to the beneficiary only against sight draft

　　　C. always advance money to the beneficiary without recourse

　　　D. advance money to the beneficiary with recourse provided that the credit is not confirmed by it

4. A credit can be negotiated by＿＿＿＿.

　　　A. the importer

　　　B. the beneficiary

　　　C. the advising bank

　　　D. the applicant of the credit or the advising bank

5. If the negotiating bank has negotiated a credit confirmed by itself, it will＿＿＿＿.

　　　A. be able to claim repayment from the beneficiary of the advance which is not ultimately forthcoming from the issuing bank

　　　B. not be able to claim repayment from he beneficiary of the advance which is not ultimately forthcoming from the issuing bank, provided the term of the credit have been complied with

　　　C. be able to claim repayment from the beneficiary of the interest which is not ultimately forthcoming from the issuing bank

　　　D. not be able to obtain reimbursement from the issuing bank

Passage Three

Consumer Credits are high risk and high interest credit products, which are

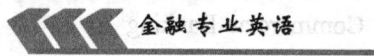

usually classified into three sorts: amortization loan, credit card and non-installment loan for purchasing cars or non-structure houses or investing a little amount and so on. Their maturity usually range from two to five years. Education loan is just one type of amortization loans.

Credit card, first issued by Franklin National Bank in 1952, is a kind of revolving loan, and is getting more and more popular.

Non-installment loan is a kind of short-term loan to meet temporary need and is supposed to pay back at one time. It is also called bridge loan.

Commercial banks provide long-term Mortgage Loans to borrowers (consumers) to purchase houses/land. The ownership of the property remains in mortgagees and the possession of property usually remains in mortgagors useless and until the occurrence of default or full repayment. Maturity of such loans is usually 30 years and the interest rates are fixed. Maximum amount of such loans is 70% of the property value, and the balance should be paid in cash as down payment. A home mortgage plan is much more than a mortgage loan. It has additional benefits. For example, the loan is up to 85% of borrower's property value, and repayment periods are up to 30 years. Repayment schemes include straight line repayment schemes, reducing balance payment schemes, step-up repayment schemes, and fortnightly repayment option. Other financial services include home owner's overdraft, up to HK $400,000, decoration loan as much as HK $400,000 with a repayment period of up to three years.

Bridging loan, which will help borrowers to complete the purchase of the new property before borrowers' receipt of safe proceeds from borrowers' existing property, equity loan, up to HK $2,000,000 for use as a deposit for a new house, or for other personal financial needs exclusive preferential interest rate.

1. Consumer Credits are high risk and high interest credit products, which are usually classified into three sorts, they are_____.

   A. amortization loan, real estate loan and mortgage loan

Chapter 5   Commercial Banking

B. amortization loan, syndicated loan and mortgage loan

C. real estate loan, amortization loan and mortgage loan

D. amortization loan, credit card and bridge loan

2. Consumer Credits can be used to extend loans to the borrower for_____.

A. purchasing cars or acquisition of a company

B. purchasing houses or financing a project

C. financing a project or a temporary imbalance of payments

D. purchasing cars or financing a person's education

3. With mortgage loans, useless and until the occurrence of default or full repayment,_____.

A. the ownership of the property remains in borrowers and the possession of property usually remains in mortgagors

B. both the ownership and the possession of the property remain in mortgagors

C. both the ownership and the possession of the property remain in mortgagees

D. the ownership of the property remains in mortgagees and the possession of property usually remains in mortgagors

4. Maturity of mortgage loans is usually_____.

A. 20 years and the interest rate are fixed

B. 30 years and the interest rate are variable

C. 30 years and the interest rate are fixed

D. 20 years and the interest rate are variable

5. According to the passage, a home mortgage loan_____.

A. is similar to a mortgage loan

B. is absolutely different from a mortgage loan

C. has more benefits than a mortgage loan

D. None of the above is correct.

135

Passage Four

Forfaiting is a method of providing non-recourse short- and medium-term finance, usually at a fixed interest rate, to facilitate trade around the world.

Non-recourse trade finance used to be a free-market, medium-term trade credit, for capital goods, arranged by a western manufacturer to an importer in an industrializing country with limited access to hard currency. The trade credit is of non-recourse and fixed rate, usually bank-granted and often evidenced by a series of negotiable bills of exchange or promissory notes repayable semi-annually.

Forfaiting normally operates like this:

The importer finds a bank or other first class institution which is willing to guarantee his liabilities. The institution is not resident in the exporter's country (and in fact would normally be resident in the importer's country).

The method of guarantee can take the following forms: an aval, whereby the guarantor endorses bills of exchange drawn on the importer, thus becoming liable on them; a separate form of guarantee of the importer's liabilities. This usually applies when promissory notes are signed by the importer, as opposed to bills of exchange being used; when the guarantor is a bank from the United States, the guarantee takes the form of a standby letter of credit whereby the American bank undertakes to honor bills of exchange drawn in the prescribed way.

The form of the guarantee is unimportant, provided the guarantee is legally binding.

Provide the guarantor is undoubted, the exporter's bank, known as the forfaitist, will discount the bills or promissory notes, i.e. will pay the exporter the face value less the discount charges. If the importer is undoubted, then the forfeit facility could be provided without the need of a guarantee from another institution.

1. Forfaiting is a method of providing non-recourse_____.

Chapter 5 Commercial Banking

A. short-term finance, normally at a variable interest rate

B. long-term finance, normally at a variable interest rate

C. medium-term finance, normally at a fixed interest rate

D. short- and medium- term finance, normally at a fixed interest rate

2. The trade credit by way of Forfaiting is provided_____.

A. with bank or other institution as a guarantor

B. only with exporter's bank as a guarantor

C. only with importer's bank as a guarantor

D. only with bank as a guarantor

3. According to the passage, the method of guarantee can take the following forms except_____.

A. endorsement of the bill of exchange

B. a standby letter of credit

C. a separate form of guarantee of the importer's liabilities, which usually applies when promissory notes are signed by the importer

D. None of the above is the form of guarantee.

4. Which of the following statements is not true?

A. An aval is used as a form of guarantee whereby the guarantor endorses bills of exchange drawn on the importer.

B. As a form of guarantor, an aval is normally used when promissory notes are signed by the importer.

C. Instead of using an aval, another form of guarantee is often used when promissory notes are signed by the importer.

D. If the guarantee is legally binding, the form of the guarantee is not important.

5. According to the passage, which of the following statements is true. The form of the guarantee is _____.

A. not important at all

B. very important

137

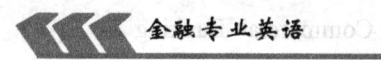金融专业英语

C. indispensable

D. sometimes not important

Passage Five

A syndicated loan is a loan arranged by a lead bank between a borrower, itself, and a group of other banks that are parties to the original credit agreement. These syndicated banks share credit agreement. These syndicated banks share credit information and credit risk.

A syndicated loan is a large credit, generally more than USD 10 million, negotiated between a borrower and a single bank, but actually funded by several other banks. The negotiating or "lead" bank has often won the "mandate" from a number of competitors and has often underwritten a large portion of the credit and is responsible for organizing the syndication. The resulting credit is governed by a single loan agreement signed by the borrower and all of the banks involved.

The syndication market has developed largely because single lenders have found it increasingly difficult to meet large borrowing requirements of corporate clients. A single bank may not be able or willing to extend such a large amount because of legal lending limits, exposure, and portfolio considerations. Also, the lead bank often chooses to allow room in its credit availability for future funding opportunities to the same borrower.

Every syndication has an agent bank to administer the loans from signing to repayment. Based on the complexity of its duties, the agent bank normally receives a fee from the borrower. This fee is separate and distinct from any front end or other fee paid to the bank. Duties of the agent include issuing advices for interest charges, processing the movement of funds, and assuring that the borrower has complied with the terms and conditions of the loan agreement.

The purpose of the syndicated loan is usually to finance a major development, a project, a temporary imbalance of payments, a major capital investment program, a project cost over-run, acquisition of a company,

138

Chapter 5 Commercial Banking

short-term to long-term debt conversion, or rationalization of its schedule of long-term debt repayments.

1. A syndicated loan is a large credit negotiated between_____.

    A. a borrower and several banks

    B. banks

    C. a borrower and a single bank

    D. None of the above is correct.

2. None of the following statements is true except_____.

    A. the lead bank in a syndicated loan is not allowed to underwrite a large portion of the credit

    B. all the banks involved in a syndicated loan must underwrite a equal portion of the credit

    C. the lead bank always underwrite a large portion of the credit

    D. the negotiating bank in a syndicated loan is also referred to as the "lead" bank

3. A single bank may not be able or willing to extend loans of large amount partly because of_____.

    A. the leading limits made by the parent of the bank

    B. the risk of the large amount loan

    C. the fact that its portfolio forbids large amount loan

    D. the fact it is impossible for a single bank to extend loans of large amount

4. The purpose of the syndicated loan is usually to provide finance to _____.

    A. a house buyer

    B. a car buyer

    C. a company to meet its temporary needs

    D. None of the above is correct.

5. The agent bank in a syndicated loan normally receives a fee_____.

A. which is similar to the front end fee

B. which is from the lead bank

C. which is paid together with front end fee

D. which is paid by the borrower

Put the following sentences into English.

1. 货款收妥后，请汇往托收委托书中所指定的银行。

2. 进口商付款之前，由银行控制货物所有权单据。

3. 随着国际贸易的发展，一些新的支付方式被采纳了。

4. 跟单信用证是进口商的银行根据进口商的要求，向出口商开立的一种银行信用工具。它包含了一项保证：即在出口商提供完全符合信用证条款的货运单据时，开证行同意付款。

5. 任何银行由于任何原因，不能按照它所接到的托收委托书指示办理时，必须立即通知托收行。

6. 银行应将收到的单据与托收委托书所列者核对一致，任何单据遗漏时，银行必须立即通知托收行。银行没有审核单据的义务。

7. 提示行应尽力查明拒绝付款或拒绝承兑的理由并将其通知托收行。

8. 银行对于货物采取保护行为所发生的费用和开支将由委托人负担。

9. 如果是凭单远期付款，当要求承兑交单时，提示行应立即提示承兑，不得延误。当要求付款交单时，提示付款不得迟于相应的到期日。

10. 当银行代客户办理托收业务，它将处理两类单据，其一是金融单据，其二是商业单据。

11. 收到你方信用证修改书后，我行已同受益人联系并得知，如果有效期再延展至 5 月 31 日，他们将接受上述修改。

12. 除非此证由第三者银行加保兑，不然受益人是不会接受该证的。

13. 在信用证业务中，有关银行只受信用证措辞的约束，但不受销售合同的约束。

Chapter 5 Commercial Banking

True or False

1. Cash in advance, open account, collection and documentary credit are the usual methods of payment to settle international trade transactions.

2. A documentary collection is an arrangement whereby the seller draws only a draft on the buyer for the value of the goods and presents the draft to his bank.

3. Credits, by the nature, are separate transactions from the sales or other contracts on which they may be based, and banks are in no way concerned wish or bound by such contracts.

4. It is documentary letter of credit that affords a high degree of safety for both buyers and sellers.

5. Under documentary letter of credit, the remitting bank has no obligation to examine documents.

6. Under documentary collection, the remitting bank has no obligation to examine documents.

7. The UCP rules have been in effect since 1923.

8. To the exporter of goods, the most satisfactory arrangement as far as payment is concerned is to receive it in advance.

9. Trade on open account arrangement usually satisfies the seller's desire for cash and the importer's desire for credit.

10. Usually the advising bank is the bank located in the same city as the buyer.

11. Drafts which are payable at a future date are called demand drafts.

12. If the instructions are D/P the importer's bank will release the documents to the importer only against payment.

13. Normally D/P will apply with sight drafts and D/A will apply with usance drafts.

14. The four main parties to a documentary collection are the principal,

the remitting bank, the collecting bank and the drawee.

15. The principal is usually the importer.
16. Promissory notes are commercial documents.
17. Banks have no liability for any delay or loss caused by postal or telex failure.
18. In the case of documents payable at sight the presenting bank must make presentation for payment without delay.
19. Banks have no obligation to take any action in respect of the goods to which a documentary collection relates.
20. Goods should not be dispatched direct to the address of a bank or consigned to a bank without prior agreement on the part of that bank.
21. The authority of the "case of need" must be specified in the collection order.
22. It is unnecessary to carry out the collection order in the case of non-payment.
23. Accepted drafts must be presented for payment on maturity.
24. A formal protest can only be made by a Notary Public.
25. A bill should be protested within one business day of dishonour.
26. A remitting bank will not accept unqualified acceptance.
27. The instructions of the drawee override the collection order.
28. Standard international rules governing the role and responsibilities of banks in collections is UCP 500.
29. A bank will handle the documents only on the basis of instructions received.
30. Acceptance must be made at the back of the bill and signed by the drawee.

Multiple Choice

1. After the goods have been shipped, the exporters present the

Chapter 5 Commercial Banking

documents to_____.

A. the remitting bank   B. the collecting bank

C. the reimbursing bank   D. the opening bank

2. The instructions for collection are mainly _____.

A. those in the contract   B. written on the Bill of Exchange

C. given by the importers   D. given by the exporters

3. An additional risk borne by the seller when granting a credit to the buyer is that the latter will not_____.

A. accept the bill   B. take up the documents

C. take delivery   D. make payment at maturity

4. The remitting bank checks the documents received_____.

A. as a service to its clients B. to avoid unnecessary

C. before sending them out   D. all of the above

5. To the exporter, the fastest and safest method of settlement is_____.

A. letter of credit   B. advance payment

C. collection   D. banker's draft

6. To the importer, the fastest and safest method of settlement is_____.

A. letter of credit   B. cash in advance

C. open account   D. banker's draft

7. Before opening a credit, the issuing bank should_____.

A. go through the contract terms

B. fill in the application form

C. sign an agreement with the customer

D. inquire into the customer's credit standing

8. The exporter can receive the payment only when_____.

A. he has shipped the goods

B. he has presented the documents

143

C. the documents presented comply with he credit terms

D. the importer has taken delivery of the goods

9. Settlement by documentary credit is fair to_____.

A. the shipping company   B. the trading companies concerned

C. the banks involved   D. All of the above

10. In credit transactions, the goods and the documents are sent to the importer_____.

A. in different ways   B. in the same way

C. in different directions   D. at one time

11. It will be more convenient if the collection bank appointed by the seller_____.

A. is a large bank

B. is the remitting bank's correspondent in the place of the importer

C. is in the exporter's country

D. acts on the importer's instructions

12. The commission charged by a third bank involved in the collection should be paid by _____.

A. the exporter   B. the importer

C. the correspondent bank   D. the remitting bank

13. The reasonable time concerning protest for non-payment or non-acceptance is usually_____.

A. half a day   B. one or two days

C. ten hours   D. twenty-four hours

14. The documents will not be delivered to the buyer until_____.

A. the goods have arrived   B. the bill is paid or accepted

C. the buyer has cleared the goods   D. Both A and B

15. The importance of distinction between financial documents and commercial documents lies in that it helps decide whether it is_____.

Chapter 5　Commercial Banking

    A. inward collection or outward collection

    B. bill collection or goods collection

    C. cash collection or check collection

    D. clean collection or documentary collection

16. The operation of collection begins with_____.

    A. the customer and the remitting bank

    B. the remitting bank and the collection bank

    C. the presenting bank and the drawee

    D. the collection bank and the presenting bank

17. Detailed instructions must be sent to the collecting bank_____.

    A. in the application form   B. in the collection order

    C. in the documents   D. Both A and B

18. Banks are obligated to verify the documents received to see that_____.

    A. they are authentic

    B. they are regular

    C. they are those listed in the collection order

    D. they are in the right form

19. The collection bank will make a protest only when_____.

    A. the documents are rejected

    B. a case of need is nominated

    C. specific instructions concerning protest are given

    D. protective measures in respect of the goods are taken

20. If it is not stated as D/A or D/P, the documents can be released_____.

    A. against payment   B. against acceptance

    C. in either way   D. against acceptance pour aval

145

Cloze Test

Passage One

Following the substantial growth of international trade, the banker's documentary letter of credit has been commonly employed. It is the documentary letter of credit that afford a high degree of____1____for both buyers and sellers. The abundant monetary resources and the high credit standing of a large bank are called in to supplement the little known financial standing and integrity of____2____. The banking aid thus enlisted is in itself a guarantee of the buyers' commercial standing and means.

While the wording of documentary credit is not____3____in all cases and may in varying degrees differ from that of the standard form, it invariably comprises the following two essential conditions under which credits are made available:

1. It always indicates the exact shipping and other document which the beneficiaries must____4____.

2. It contains clear indication on the part of ____5____that they irrevocably undertake to honour the shipping and other documents presented by he beneficiaries when they ____6____the terms and conditions mentioned in the credit.

Passage Two

Documentary collection is the handling of commercial documents whether or not accompanied____1____for payment, acceptance or delivery as the instructions received.

Documentary collection is a service provided by banks, whereby the seller/exporter____2____the goods, ____3____the documents to his bank (remitting bank) with instructions to have the documents presented to the buyer/importer through a bank (collecting bank) in the country of ____4____. The collecting bank is obliged to deliver the shipping documents, particularly the document of title

Chapter 5   Commercial Banking

to goods to the buyer/importer only ___5___ the instructions of the remitting bank. The instructions of the remitting bank are basically those of the seller/exporter. Generally, the instructions would be to release the documents only ___6___ payment of the amount due or acceptance of a tenor bill of exchange if credit has been granted by the seller/exporter.

The bill for collection service is suitable for securing payment for delivery or shipment made to trustworthy buyers/importers. A bill for collection gives a fair degree of control ___7___ the shipping documents as the collecting bank is authorised to release the same only upon payment, or acceptance. Where the seller/exporter extends credit to the buyer/importer and instructs that documents may be released upon acceptance of a bill of exchange, he face an additional risk in that the buyer/importer may accept the bill of exchange, take up the documents, clear the goods but subsequently ___8___ payment on maturity date of the bill of exchange.

Passage Three

Thus, from the borrower's ___1___ , syndication in both the domestic and international markets allows for the efficient arrangement of a larger amount of funds than any single lender can feasibly supply.

In the Eurocurrency market, however, syndicated lending becomes less of a convenience and ___2___ of a necessity. The need to finance balance of payment deficits, coupled with the lack of ___3___ financing arrangements in external markets, creates a demand for huge bank loans by country borrowers. In the U.S. domestic market, if a business needs a large amount of long-term ___4___ , bank loans are only one of several options. The firm may also arrange for bond or equity issue. In external markets, however, there are fewer options, and moreover they may not be ___5___ to borrowers from less-developed countries. Industrial country borrowers, both governmental and private, may have access to the international bond markets, but borrowers from less-developed countries generally do not. Thus the only available source of financing for the latter group may be the syndicated Eurocurrency loan market.

1. A. view   B. aspect   C. viewpoint   D. point

2. A. more   B. less   C. few   D. much

3. A. the other   B. another   C. more   D. alternative

4. A. cash   B. funding   C. capital   D. borrowing

5. A. available   B. ready   C. allowed   D. suitable

Chapter 6
Investment Banking

6.1　Investment Banking

Investment banks and investment banking are now among the top agenda of politicians, industrialists, finance regulators and students of financial systems. The sector's rapid expansion in size and geographical coverage, changes in its scope, and its impact on the structure of the economy and financial system, pose important questions.

We hereby present in this chapter a brief introduction of the investment banking industry—its main features, basic functions, historical development, as well as how it is distinguished from the commercial banking. However, as such a rapid developing industry it is, to present the latest features and innovations in this industry would be a mission too hard for this book. So it would be a good idea to get a basic map of investment banking in this chapter, and to get a full exposure in the real economic life and financial system.

6.2　Backgrounds

Investment banks are financial institutions engaged in investment banking activities. Investment banking are banking activities associated with securities underwriting, making a market in securities, and arranging mergers, acquisitions and restructuring.

Investment banking is a highly specialized segment of finance industry. Its basic function is to bring together, directly through the mechanism of financial markets, ultimate savers and saving-collecting institutions with those wishing to raise additional funds for investment or consumption. It also facilitates holders of accumulated wealth, held in the form of financial instruments, to re-allocate their assets using financial markets in accordance with their changing evaluation of the attraction of the combination of risk/reward/liquidity attributes of individual financial assets, compared with each other and with real assets. In performing these two basic functions those involved in investment banking act as market intermediaries.

Investment banks must be distinguished from commercial banks and other savings-collecting institutions who gather and decide themselves on the allocation of savings and who act as financial intermediaries. The use of financial markets is thus at the heart of investment banking. Its development and evolution have been closely linked to the growth and expansion of financial markets (and above all capital markets), the instruments they employ and the mechanisms they use.

There is an important distinction between the activity of investment banking and the institutions that perform it. Investment banking activity can be, and is also undertaken by, banks (who are financial intermediaries), provided that the respective regulatory framework allow it and an individual bank's (i,e. universal banks) wish to engage in it. Indeed, the history of the development of investment banking is the history of deposit and commercial banks moving into this field, subject to regulatory constrains.

Investment banking activities are undertaken by specialized and independent investment banking institutions offering all or some of the services described above, or by universal banks alongside their traditional deposit-taking and loan business. The type of institution engaged in investment banking is determined by regulatory framework within which financial institutions are free to operate at any particular time within these frontiers by the choice by individual institutions of their preferred segments and produces.

Broadly speaking one can say that there are two types of regulatory framework. The first allows investment banking to be carried out by all types commercial banks, resulting in the emergence of universal bank which, alongside commercial banking, engaged in all or some types of investment banking. The second approach separates classic investment banking (i. e. underwriting) from commercial banking and sometimes also other types of investment banking activities.

6.3   Investment Banks and Financial System

In as much as investment banking enables the financial system to perform some of its basic functions better and more efficiently, its evolution is one of the important factors propelling the development of the financial system as a whole. The fundamental functions that the financial system must perform are, first, to run and manage the payment clearance and settlement system; second, to provide liquidity; third, to transfer savings from surplus units to deficit units and allocate these according to respective risk / reward / liquidity preferences; fourth, to monitor and discipline units using externally raised funds; and finally, to price, transfer and trade risks.

Investment banking can be said to stimulate the pace of transformation of the system in that it helps to move it from a bank-orientated system, where all five functions are performed by commercial banks by way of bilateral agreements, to the market-orientated phase, where markets play an increasing role in the performance of the last three functions and then to phase where markets and investment banking dominate the financial system. This path of progress is economically beneficial as it reduce the resources employed to perform some of these basic functions; it improves quality in that it improves the

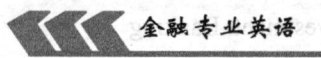

risk evaluation, risk sharing and risk diversifying functions; and, finally by increasing scope it enhances the ability of an economy to carry more risk and to respond more rapidly to changes and to take remedial action in relation to the performance of units using externally raised funds.

6.4   Investment Banking Activities

Because of the changing trends discussed above, investment banking today is separated into three distinct activities: underwriting, or the new issue of securities; transactions, including trading in the secondary market, proprietary trading for the firm's own account, and retail brokerage; and fee banking, involving activities earning a fee such as advising on mergers and acquisitions, securities and economic research, and other types of financial consulting. But simple distinction can be difficult to maintain. Advising client on a potential acquisition requires an investment bank to perform certain activities in the primary or secondary market, or both. Some institutions may call that activity mergers and acquisitions while others may call it cooperate finance.

1. Underwriting New Issue

New securities issued by companies are usually brought to market after advice and a commitment to underwrite by an investment banking firm. Underwriting simply means that the investment banker promises to buy the securities. The investment bank helps design the security and they buys it from the issuer with intent of selling it to investors as quickly as possible.

2. Mergers and Acquisitions

Mergers and acquisitions simply mean that one company would attempt to take over another by gaining enough of its common stock to gain control. In the simplest sense, merger means two companies becoming one with the acquirer

Chapter 6   Investment Banking

being in the commanding position.

Another type of merger, or takeover as the case may be, is the merger of two unrelated companies. This is known as the conglomerate merger—a company purposely buying another not engaged in the same business at all.

6.5   Prospect of Investment Banking

Looking ahead the economic factors is likely to continue to extend their influence in favor of expansion of investment banking, and changes in the financial system regulatory framework will inevitably follow them. Globalization of the world economy can be expected to lead to a rise in the relative importance of investment banking in the financial system. The attention paid to and the need to contain systemic risks are likely to accelerate this trend, placing financial markets and investment banking even more firmly at the center of finance and banking.

参考译文

第6章 投资银行

6.1 投资银行

投资银行和投资银行业务现在已经成为政治家、实业家以及金融机构的最重要的议事日程安排，也是金融体系重要的内容。投资银行业务规模不断膨胀，业务范围也不断在向更多的地域覆盖，与此同时，投资银行领域内自身也在发生着日新月异的变化，这一切都给当今世界的金融体系和经济结构带来了深刻的变化和影响，同时也在不断提出新的问题。

在本章中将简要介绍投资银行业务，内容包括投资银行业务的主要特征、基本功能和发展历史，以及它如何从传统的商业银行业务中分离出来的。但是，投资银行业务发展变化得非常迅速，因此要想在本书中介绍当前它最新的特征与创新比较困难。所以，本章只阐述投资银行业务发展的大体状况，读者自行从真实的经济生活和金融体系中了解它的全貌。

6.2 背景

投资银行是专门从事投资银行业务的金融机构。投资银行业务是指涉及证券承销业务、证券市场业务、公司资产兼并重组业务等方面的金融活动。

投资银行业务是金融领域内高度专业化的部分。第一，投资银行通过各种金融机构，为市场中的最终存款者和储蓄银行之间建立了联系，储蓄银行通过投资银行可以扩大自己的融资渠道。第二，当市场中财富拥有者希望对自己的资产进行重新安排，来改变原有财产的风险/回报/流动性特征时，投资银行就可以通过向这些客户提供自己的各种金融工具和金融产品以满足其要求。投资银行的这两项基本功能体现了投资银行作为金融中介机构的特点。

投资银行与传统的商业银行不同之处在于，传统商业银行可以将自己吸收的存款进行信贷分配，而投资银行与储蓄吸纳银行不同之处在于，储蓄银行仅仅是一个金融中介。投资银行的核心业务就是要运用各种金融工具参与到金融市场的活动中。投资业务的发展和演变与金融市场的发展增长以及投资银行所使用的金融工具机制密切相关。

投资银行的业务与从事投资银行业务的金融机构之间有重要的区别。一般是由银行(金融中介机构)来从事投资银行业务，但如果有关法律允许，或者某家综合性银行愿意介入投资银行业务，可以由它们来从事投资银行业务。事实上，投资银行的发展是伴随着商业银行和储蓄银行在从事该领域的过程中不断受限制而发展起来的。

投资银行业务既可以由那些独立、专业的投资银行机构来提供，也可以由那些同时从事传统的存贷款业务的全能银行来提供。从事投资银行业务的机构的类型往往取决于金融体系中金融监管机制的不同，在不同监管机制下，会产生不同类型的机构，在特定时间从事特定的投资银行业务。

一般来说有两种类型的金融监管框架。在第一种监管框架下，它允许各种类型的商业银行从事投资银行业务，因此在此框架下，随着业务的不断发展，也就产生了全能银行，可以同时从事投资银行业务和传统商业银行业务。在第二种监管框架下，它将典型的投资银行业务(比如说证券承销业务)从一般商业银行业务或者其他类型的投资银行业务中剥离出来，使其由专业投资银行机构来从事。

6.3 投资银行与金融体系

由于投资银行业务的产生与发展使金融系统可以更好、更有效地发挥其基本的资金配置功能，因此投资银行业务自身的发展也是促进当前金融体系发展的一个重要因素。金融体系的基本功能如下：第一，提供完善的支付与结算机制；第二，提供流动性；第三，在资金盈余者与稀缺者之间进行资金配置，同时使得其各自的风险/收益/流动性要相匹配；第四，对从外部筹集资金的经济主体要进行监管；最后，对风险要进行定价和管理。

在传统的银行导向型的体系下，商业银行通过双边协议的方式来发挥以上所提到的五种主要的功能。而投资银行业务的出现使得金融体系由银行导向型向市场导向型发展的步伐加快了。在市场导向型的金融体系下，市场在发挥后三个功能上的作用越来越重要了，另外，在此体系下，市场和投资银行主导了整个金融体系。这个变化发展也同时降低了原先基础功能上的人力资源的消耗，它提高了风险评估、风险分散与管理的质量，最后，通过其业务领域的拓展，投资银行业务也提高了经济体抵御风险的能力，增强了经济主体对变化的适应调整能力，同时也改善了那些通过外部融资的企业的业绩。

6.4 投资银行业务

由于上述主要的变化趋势，投资银行业务如今被分成三个不同的独立的组成部分：证券承销业务或称证券发行业务；交易业务，包括在二级资本市场上的证券买卖业务、证券自营业务和零售经纪业务；银行的基本收费服务业务，包括兼并和收购业务的咨询服务，证券与经济研究咨询业务以及其他类型的金融咨询服务。以上业务要完全加以区别是不容易的。对潜在收购进行咨询的客户往往也可能需要投资银行为他们在一级或二级市场从事一定的金融活动。不同的机构对此称呼也不同，有些称作兼并与收购，也有机构称作公司金融。

1. 增资承销

公司在资本市场上进行增资发行新股时往往都要先与投资银行就此业务进行咨询，然后再签订一个证券承销合同。投资银行同意承销意味着它承诺将买进发行人的证券。投资银行帮助上市公司设计发行方案，然后由它将证券从上市公司处买进后，再尽快在市场上向一般投资者出售。

2. 兼并与收购

兼并简单来说就是一家公司通过购买其他公司的普通股股票从而来实

现对此公司的控制。再简单来说，即两家公司通过其中一家公司的收购行为而成为一家公司，收购公司将来会有控制权。

另一种类型的兼并发生在两家不相关的公司之间。也就是说，一家公司收购另一家业务与本公司不同的企业来完成产业间的集聚发展。

6.5 投资银行前景

回首投资银行的发展历程，投资银行由于其自身独特的经济优势决定其势必将继续发展，由此带来的金融体系监管机制的变化也是不可避免的。经济全球化将会使投资银行在金融体系中的作用越来越重要。加强对系统风险的防范也会加剧投资银行发展的趋势，因此金融市场和投资银行将会成为未来的金融体系的中心。

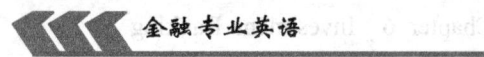

Subject Topic(命题对话)

Monetary Policy and Economic Adjustments
(货币政策与经济调整)

A: Can you tell me why we need to make some slight economic adjustments while we continue to keep our monetary policy moderately tightened?

B: Well, what you have mentioned is one of the central bank's mid-term policies. With a moderately tightened monetary policy, we gain some flexibility when we regulate the economy. The central bank will adjust the degree of tightness under different conditions. If there were an economic deflation, the central bank would lower the degree of tightness to stimulate domestic demand. If there were economic inflation, the central bank would do the reverse.

Right now in China, the conditions for economic development are not very favorable. State-owned enterprises have a lot of difficulties because the market has turned into a buyer's market. China's export competitiveness has been greatly weakened because of the Asian financial crisis. The development of township enterprises has slowed down. The growth rate of these enterprises has fallen from 30% to 10%. With all these unfavorable factors, it is not an easy task to achieve the 8% growth rate as we planned. Therefore, we need to increase the money supply moderately to stimulate effective demand so as to promote economic growth.

A: As we know, the central bank has reduced the interest rates three times in 1998. Do you know the reasons for that?

B: Actually there are many reasons for that. First, since the beginning of 1998, the price index has been dropping, and as a result the real interest rate has gone up continuously. This phenomenon hinders economic development. Second, the reduced interest rates will lighten the interest burden of some

Chapter 6　Investment Banking

enterprises, especially.

Questions and Answers(专业问答)

1. Which does commercial bank's liabilities operation mainly have?

　—It has deposits, accounts payable, shareholder's equity, etc..

2. Which does commercial bank's assets operation mainly have?

　— It has cash, loans, bill discounts, investments, etc..

3. What is the operation objective of commercial bank?

　—It is profit.

4. What are the management principles of commercial bank?

　—They are profitability, safety and liquidity.

5. What are the basic principles of letter of credit?

　—They are :

　　a. The issuing bank assumes primary payment liability.

　　b. The issuing bank must make sure that the documents presented are in conformity with the conditions of the credit while performing payment liability.

　　c. L/C originates from basic contract, but is independent of it.

Exercises(练习)

Cloze Test

Investment institutions _____1_____ the third major category in our financial system. These institutions combine the relatively small amounts of savings from many individuals and invest the _____2_____ in financial assets. Mutual funds purchase corporate stocks and bonds as well as government securities. Real estate investment trusts invest in _____3_____ and mortgages.

159

Money market funds invest in short-term debt securities. While individual investors can invest directly in such securities, investment institutions _____4_____ small investors diversification and experienced management of their funds. The fourth category consists of financial companies. These companies provide loans directly to consumers and businesses. Sales and consumer finance companies lend to individuals. Sale finance companies finance installment loan purchases of automobiles and other _____5_____ goods. Consumer finance companies provide small loans to individuals and households. The fifth category consists of securities market institutions that are involved in the savings-investment process and the marketing and transferring of claims to wealth. Credit-reporting and credit-rating organizations aid lenders in deciding whether to extend credit to consumers and businesses.

      1. A. found   B. set up   C. establish   D. make up

      2. A. money   B. total   C. final   D. amount

      3. A. stocks   B. property   C. asset   D. houses

      4. A. offer   B. provide   C. produce   D. deliver

      5. A. tangible   B. family   C. industrial   D. durable

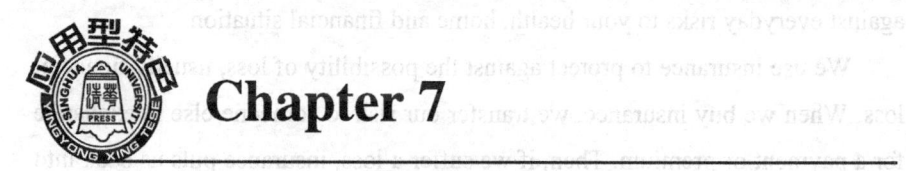

Chapter 7

Insurance

7.1 What Is Insurance and How It Works?

Risk exists when there is uncertainty about the future. Both individuals and businesses experience two kinds of risk—speculative risk and pure risk. Speculative risk involves three possible outcomes: loss, gain, or no change. For example, when you purchase shares of stock, you are speculating that the value of the stock will rise and that you will earn a profit on your investment. At the same time, you know that the value of the stock could fall and that you lose some or all of the money you invested. Finally, you know that the value of the stock could remain the same—you might not lose money, but you might not make a profit.

Pure risk involves no possibility of gain, either a loss occurs or no loss occurs. An example of pure risk is the possibility that you may become disabled. If you are unable to work, you will experience a financial loss. If, on the other hand, you never become disabled, then you will incur no loss from that risk. This possibility of financial loss without the possibility of gain—pure risk—is the only kind of risk that can be insured. The purpose of insurance is to compensate for financial loss, not to provide an opportunity for financial gain.

Insurance is a precaution against a possible unwanted outcome: in life and in business, it's a way of managing risk and keeping things on the move. In simple terms, insurance allows someone who suffers a loss or accident to be compensated for the effects of their misfortune. It lets you protect yourself against everyday risks to your health, home and financial situation.

We use insurance to protect against the possibility of loss, usually financial loss. When we buy insurance, we transfer our risk to someone else in exchange for a payment or premium. Then, if we suffer a loss, insurance puts us back into a position pre-claim (reinstatement).

And if you think about it, nothing happens without insurance! We couldn't run businesses or drive cars, own homes or travel anywhere without it, because the potential risks would be too great. Insurance gives us the peace of mind and security we need to operate.

It works because insurance companies group gather a large number of people who all feel exposed to the same possible circumstances. The company knows that, in any one year, the total premium collected from the group of people should cover the cost of the claims made by the unfortunate few who actually suffer a loss. That's to say, insurance spreads the risk of financial loss among a great many people. There are two important factors here:

1. Many people share the risk.

The insurance company collects the small amounts of money from many people and adds them together to create a large pool of funds. This pool of money is what the insurance company uses to make the very large payments to the people who suffer catastrophic losses. The risk of loss is spread over a large number of people.

2. Losses do not happen all at once.

Events that are covered by insurance do not all happen on the same day of the year. They are spread out more or less evenly over the whole year. This means that the insurance company collects the money from the many before it has to pay it out to the few.

Insurance companies invest this pool of money in the money and capital markets. They make mortgage loans and buy bonds, stocks and money market instruments. The interest, dividends and capital gains that they earn on these

Chapter 7 Insurance

investments are added to the pool of money from the premiums.

This means that there is more money available to pay the few than just what was collected from the many. Therefore, the premiums the many pay are lower than they would otherwise be. Investment income of insurance companies means lower premium payments by people buying insurance.

7.2 The Types of Insurance

There are many different types of insurance:

1. Life insurance: Money paid in the event of the death of the insured.

2. Health insurance: Money paid for doctors, nurses, medications, hospital care in case the insured becomes sick or injured.

3. Accident insurance: Money paid in the event the insured loses one or more body parts or is killed in an accident.

4. Property insurance: Money paid in the event that property is lost, damaged or stolen.

5. Liability insurance: Money paid in the event that the insured cause damage to someone else's person or property.

7.3 The Fundamentals of Insurance

Insurance is a formal, legally binding contract between the insurance company and the individual or organization buying the insurance. This contract is called a policy and the purchaser of the insurance is called a policyholder, also called the owner of the insurance policy. The owner is usually the insured person, but it may also be a relative of the insured, a partnership or a corporation. All rights, benefits and privileges under insurance policies are controlled by their owners. Ownership may be assigned or transferred by the owner to

163

someone else.

When an event occurs that is covered by an insurance policy, the insurance company pays the amount specified in the policy for the loss related to that type of event. The person (or organization) to whom the insurance proceeds are to be paid in the event of a loss is called the "beneficiary" in the case of life insurance and the "loss payee" in the case of property insurance.

One of the most important points to remember is that the client must have an insurable interest. Otherwise a contract of insurance will not be issued. This means that the person (or organization) to whom the insurance proceeds are to be paid if and when the specific event occurs must suffer a financial loss in proportion to the amount of insurance. Generally, an insurable interest must be demonstrated when a policy is issued and in the case of property insurance, must exist at the time of a loss. Once a life insurance policy has been issued, the insurer must pay the policy benefit, whether or not an insurable interest continues to exist.

A typical insurance policy usually contains such details as follows: the amount insured; the amount of each premium payment to be made by the policyholder; when and how often premium payment are to be made; the risks covered—what events the insurance will pay for; how much the insurance company will pay in respect of each occurrence of an event that is covered by the policy; and what the policyholder must do(or not do) in order to keep the insurance in force.

Once the event covered by insurance policy has occurred, the policyholder or beneficiary should notify the insurance company timely. The company's representative, called a claims adjuster, will ask some details about the event and the amount of the loss. The policyholder(beneficiary) will also be asked to fill out a claim form which provide the insurance company with the details it requires and swear that the information is true and correct in all respects. Once the claims adjuster confirms it, a cheque for the portion covered by the insurance

Chapter 7　Insurance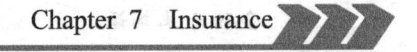

company will be sent to the policyholder(beneficiary) in several days.

7.4　Legal Principles of Insurance

There are four legal principles of insurance: principle of indemnity, principle of insurance interests, principle of subrogation, and principle of utmost good faith.

7.4.1　Principle of Indemnity

Principle of indemnity is usually contained in all insurance contracts for it is a legal base. Therefore in the event of a loss of the scope of insurance coverage, insurance policy holders will obtain the value of the loss which will not exceed the actual cash value. It should be borne in mind that the value lost is usually decided at the moment of loss. This principle could prevent insurance policy holders from using claim to make profit.

7.4.2　Principle of Insurance Interests

To be an enforceable insurance contract, an insurance policy should meet the following needs: The insured risk-bearing entity should have the insurable interest, the main body of the insured and the insured risk should be included in insurance policies, and the insured entities should be faced with economic loss or other damage to danger, which should be included in the insurance agreement, the terms and conditions of the various losses in insurance policy. This is the principle of insurance interests.

Particularly in the fields of property and liability insurance, insurable interest is every interest in property or potential loss of assets arising out of legal liability of such a nature that a contemplated peril may result in an economic loss to the injured. The foregoing definition should be interpreted to include the

165

 金融专业英语

following: (1) ownership or possession, (2) liability or bailee, (3) creditor-debtor, (4) contractual interests, (5) expectation (with qualification).

In the broad sense, an insurable interest implies some relationship between the insured and the event insured against, so that its occurrence would result in injury or loss. It follows that every person who has an insurable interest in property has the option to insure the same under an appropriate property or liability insurance policy. Insurable interest may assume literally hundreds of forms. Each year, new types of interests are identified and complementary insurance coverages are introduced to meet the public needs.

7.4.3 Principle of Subrogation

The principle of subrogation grows out of the principle of indemnity. Under the principle of subrogation, one who has indemnified another's loss is entitled to recovery from any liable third parties who are responsible. Thus if D negligently causes danger to E's property, E's insurance company will indemnify E to the extent of its liability for E's loss and then have the right to proceed against D for any amounts it has paid out under E's policy. One of the important reasons for subrogation is to reinforce the principle of indemnity—that is, to prevent the insured from collecting more than the actual cash loss. If E's insurer did not have the right of subrogation, it would be possible for E to recover from the policy and then recover again in a legal action against D. In this way, E would collect twice. It would be possible for E to arrange an accident with D, collect twice, and split the profit with D. A moral hazard would exist, and the contract would tend to become an instrument of fraud.

Another reason for subrogation is that it may hold rates below what they would otherwise be. In some lines of insurance, particularly liability, recoveries from negligent parties through subrogation are substantial. While no specific provision for subrogation recoveries is made in the rate structure other than through those provisions relating to salvage, the rates would tend to be higher if

166

Chapter 7 Insurance

such recoveries were not permitted. A final reason for subrogation is that the burden of loss is more nearly placed on the shoulders of those responsible. The negligent should not escape penalty because of the insurance mechanism.

7.4.4 Principle of Utmost Good Faith

This principle imposes a higher standard of honesty on parties to an insurance agreement than is imposed in ordinary commercial contracts. The principle of utmost good faith requires the real-related material of the insured or applicant, in order to help insurance companies to consider the appropriateness and acceptance of insurance. Once the material facts of security risks are found misrepresented by the applicant or insured, insurance can be declared null and void, as never happened before, so that coverage will be denied and there will be no compensation.

7.5 Insurance Market

Insurance market is a place that insurance trading happens as well as a mechanism that all types of factors participating in the insurance commodity trading interacts.

There are two participants in insurance market: the supplier and the the buyer. Most insurance is provided by corporations. Some are owned by policyholders themselves, others are owned by government. In recent years, many commercial banks have set up their own insurance companies in order to participate in this attractive and growing market. At the same time, individuals, families, businesses, organizations and governments all buy insurance.

Insurance could be bought through the following two ways: directly with an insurance company or indirectly through an intermediary (such as insurance broker or insurance agents). The insurance applicant must pay the premium for insurance. The premium is the amount the insurance company charges the

167

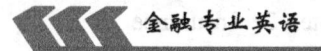 金融专业英语

insured for assuming the risk of loss. The insurance company calculates the premium by determining the likelihood of that a particular loss will occur and then applying that probability to the amount to be paid out if the event triggering the loss does occur.

For an insurance applicant, buying insurance comes about in one of two ways: the initiatives comes from the prospective buyer or the seller (insurance company representative). At the first meeting, the insurance representative will concentrate on understanding the prospective client's situation, needs and objectives. This process is called a "needs analysis". Attention would be focused first on what difficulties the prospective client and family members (if any) would face if one or more particular events were to occur. These are the risks that need to be covered. Next would come a detailed evaluation of the client's personal situation and finally an exploration of goals and objectives. What is the client trying to achieve financially and how can insurance help in the realization of that dream? The representative would then structure an insurance package that would best meet the client's objectives and provide the appropriate level of protection for the identified risks. After the meeting, the insurance representative will write up an insurance proposal containing a description of the risks to be covered, the amount of protection needed, the form of insurance desired and detailed personal information about the prospective client. If the insurance representative is an independent broker, he or she will send the proposal to several insurance companies in order to obtain the lowest price. If the representative works for an agent of a particular company, he or she will forward the proposal to that company's underwriting department. The insurance company's underwriting department will review the details of the proposal. If it considers the risk acceptable, it will provide a quote to the representative—what the premium would be for the coverage desired. The representative will report the good news to the prospective client. If the price quoted is acceptable, the client will make whatever payment is required and a policy of insurance will be issued.

168

Chapter 7 Insurance

参考译文

第7章 保 险

7.1 保险的含义以及保险的运作原理

风险是指对未来事件的不确定性。个人与企业都会面临两种类型的风险——投机风险和纯粹风险。投机风险是指会产生三种可能的结果：损失、获利或无损失。举例来说，当你在购进一定份额的股票时，你可能通过自己的股票市价上涨从而获得一定的利润，也可能你的股票市价下降，那样你最初投入的资金有可能会亏损。最终，你在股市的投资总额可能不会发生变化，可能既没有亏损也没有盈利。

纯粹风险是指没有获利可能性，只有损失的可能性或者没有损失的可能性两种。纯粹风险的一个典型例子是你可能会丧失劳动力，这时你失去工作将会是你的经济损失，换句话说，如果你身体健全，你就不会失去工作，也就不会有经济损失。只有纯粹风险才是可以保险的，它只是补偿受害人的经济损失，而不是提供获利的可能性。

保险是针对未来生活或工作中可能遭遇到的不可预知的损失进行一种预防管理的措施。保险也是风险管理中的一种方法。简单来说，保险向那些遭遇到风险而受损失的人们提供了一定的损失补偿服务。因此，通过保险服务，你可以将自己生活或工作中遭遇到的身体健康、财务危机等各种风险进行分散处理，从而保障自己的经济利益。

我们通过购买保险来弥补自己可能遭受的损失，这种损失通常是一种经济损失，也即可以用货币衡量的损失。当我们购买了保险，我们所面临的某种特定风险也即被转移和分散，通常我们未来获得的保障要大大高于我们所缴纳的保费。如果未来我们遭遇到此特定风险，那么我们就可以依据保险条款向保险人提出索赔。

如果仔细考虑一下，你将会发现我们的生活中如果没有保险，可能一

169

切都无法正常运转了。我们有可能不会再从事商业经营，不能驾驶车辆，不能购置房产，也不敢去放松心情领略各地的风土人情，因为当我们做出这些行为时，通常都会面临着较大的风险。而保险服务可以在一定程度上降低我们的担忧，为上述活动提供一定程度的安全保障。

保险公司之所以能够向客户提供风险保障服务，就是因为通过大量的客户参保，保险公司将大量的面临相似风险的人群聚集在一起。而所有参保人群所交纳的保费通常会高于保险公司最终向参保人群中不幸遭受损失的人们提供的赔偿费用。也就是说，保险公司通过大量承保，将财务风险大大地分散。保险公司盈利的两个重要因素如下。

(1) 大量的同质的风险标的。

保险公司向那些可能面临相同风险的人们收取同样的少许保险费用，并将这些保险费用积聚成一个数额较大的风险保障基金，用此向其中真正不幸的受险人来进行支付，弥补其损失，因此个体的损失被参保集体中的每个人共同分担了。

(2) 风险不会同时发生。

保险公司的可保风险通常不会在保险期间内同时发生，它们或多或少地会在一年中分散发生。也就是说，保险公司通常是在风险发生、进行实际赔付之前就可以收入大量的保费。

保险公司可以将收取的保险费在货币或资本市场上进行投资。通常来说，他们可以用来发放抵押贷款，购买债券、股票或其他的货币市场投资工具。通过以上投资，保险公司可以获取分红、利息收入和资本性收入，从而能保证其保障资金能够保值、增值。

这也就意味着在将来发生实际损失要保险公司进行赔付时，保险公司能够有更加雄厚的资金实力来保障自己的偿付能力，这也是保险公司能够保持正常运营的一个重要条件。保险公司通过各种投资手段获取的资金越多，那么它向投保人征收的保险费也就可能越低。

7.2 保险类型

保险可以分为以下几种类型。

(1) 人寿保险

通常是以人的生命作为保险标的，以被保险人的死亡作为保险事故的险种。

(2) 健康保险

通常是以人的身体健康作为保险标的，对被保险人因病或因伤治疗而发生的门诊费用、护理费用、医药费用、住院费用等进行偿付。

(3) 意外保险

是指对被保险人因遭受意外事故而导致的身体伤残或死亡来进行偿付的保险。

(4) 财产保险

对被保险人的财产损失或者财产被窃来进行赔偿的保险。

(5) 责任保险

保险公司对被保险人因某些原因而导致的对第三者的人身伤害或财产损失的赔偿责任来进行赔付的保险。

7.3 保险的基本原则

保险本质上来说是保险公司与投保人(个人或法人)之间的一种正式的法律合同契约。这份保险合同称为保险单，购买保险的主体称为投保人或保险客户，也可以称为保单所有人。通常，保单所有人也就是保险中的被保险人，也可能是被保险人的亲属、合作伙伴，或者是社团、法人团体等。保单所有人拥有保单中所载明的各种权益、收益和特许权。保单所有权可以经保单所有人同意进行转让。

当保单中的保险事故发生时，保险公司将会依照保单规定支付一笔保险金。在人身保险中，从保险公司获得保险赔偿金的通常称为受益人；而在财产保险中，获取保险赔偿金的称为损失收款人。

一个非常重要的地方就是投保人必须具有可保利益。否则，该投保人不可能获得保险公司的承保。这意味着个人或组织如果希望在特定事件发生时获得保险赔偿，就必须根据保险金额支付一定比例的费用。一般来说，保险利益原则可以这样来表达，在财产保险中，投保人或被保险人必须在整个保险期间内对保险标的具有可保利益，而在人身保险中，我们只要求投保人对被保险人在投保时具有保险利益，而在保险期间内，这种保险利益是可以发生变化的。

一张典型的保险单通常包括如下细节内容：保险金额，保费，保费的支付时间和支付方式，保险责任，每次保险事故发生时保险公司支付的保险限额，投保人或保单所有人的义务。

一旦保险合同中的保险事故发生时，保单所有人或受益人应该及时通知保险公司。保险公司的代表(通常被称为索赔调理员)将会调查事故发生的具体细节以及事故损失程度，从而决定是否理赔以及理赔的程度。通常，在这种情形下，保险公司会要求保单所有人或受益人来填写一份索赔单，在此份索赔单中，受益人必须如实填写保险事故发生的具体细节内容，并力求各项内容准确无误，以便保险公司作出正确的理赔决定。一旦经过保险索赔调理员的确认，保险公司将会在几天之后向受益人进行偿付。

7.4 保险的法律原则

保险有四大基本法律原则：损失补偿原则、保险利益原则、代位求偿原则和最大诚信原则。

7.4.1 损失补偿原则

损失补偿原则通常适用于所有的保险合同，因为它是法律基础。因此，在保险责任范围内的保险事故发生时，保险公司向保险单持有人所偿付的金额是用来弥补其经济损失的，因此是以损失为限的，也是不会超过其实际现金价值的。必须注意的是，损失的价值通常是按照损失发生的时间来进行衡量的，采取这个基本原则的主要目的是防止投保人通过保险来获取收益。

7.4.2 可保利益原则(保险利益原则)

作为一个可执行的保险合同，保险单必须满足以下条件和要求：在签订和履行保险合同的过程中，投保人和被保险人对保险标的必须具有法律上承认的利益，否则保险合同无效。换言之，如果损失发生，被保险人必须在经济上遭受损失，或者必须遭受其他种类的损害。保险协议中必须记载保险公司可以承担的各种类型的风险损失。这就是保险的保险利益原则。

在财产保险和责任保险中，保险利益是指保单所有人或投保人因为其财产或资产利益遭受到各种未知的风险而引起的经济损失。具体来说，可保利益可以概括为如下几点：

(1) 财产所有权人或经营管理人的保险利益；

(2) 债权人或财产保管人的保险利益；

(3) 债权-债务人的保险利益；

(4) 合同双方当事人的保险利益；

(5) 预期利益。

宽泛地讲，保险利益原则实际上也就暗示了被保险人与保险事故之间存在某种特定的关系，这种关系意味着保险事故发生就会带来某种损失。因此我们也可以得出如下结论，那就是对某一特定财产具有可保利益的任何人都可以为该财产投保财产险或者责任险。保险利益形式多样。每一年，都会有新兴的保险利益出现，因此保险公司也必须对自己的产品进行不断的更新来适应公众的新需求。

7.4.3 代位求偿原则

代位求偿原则是损失补偿原则的派生原则。在代位求偿原则下，当保险标的是由第三者责任导致的损失时，保险公司按照合同约定履行赔偿责任后，依法将取得对保险标的的所有权或者对保险标的的损失负有责任的第三者的追偿权。举例来说，如果 D 由于自己的疏忽或过失造成了 E 的损失，E 的保险公司在依据保险合同规定对 E 的财产损失进行赔偿以后，E 的保险公司就取得 E 向 D 请求的损失赔偿权，也即 E 的保险公司可以要求 D 对保险公司向 E 赔付的部分进行赔偿。代位求偿原则实际上是对损失赔偿原则的一个修订或者说是补充规定，也就是说当被保险人 E 从保险公司处获得赔偿以后，被保险人 E 就无权就所获赔偿部分向第三方 D 再次请求赔偿，从而防止了被保险人 E 双倍获偿，进而获取利润。因此，E 可能和 D 合谋，制造事故，双倍获偿后与 D 分赃。如果没有代位求偿原则的规定，就有可能产生道德风险，保险合同也会成为某些人欺诈骗保的工具。

代位求偿的另一个原因是它的追回比率比较低。在一些保险公司的业务中，特别是义务的履行，过失方通过代位求偿来追回补偿的占多数。当代位求偿没有特定的条款时，追回是以比率来计算的，而不是根据有关救助的条款来计算。如果不是用这种方法，追回的比率将会高一些。代位求偿的最后一个原因是损失的负担将更多地加在责任一方身上，因为保险的机制不会让这种过失的责任方逃脱惩罚。

7.4.4 最大诚信原则

最大诚信原则要求保险合同的当事人必须以最大的诚意履行自己应尽的义务，互不欺骗和隐瞒。与其他经济合同比较而言，保险合同的双方必须表现高度诚实。最大诚信原则要求被保险人或者投保人必须将投保的相关信息如实准确地告知保险公司，保险公司可以据此决定是否承保以及承保的具体内容。当保险人发现投保人或被保险人未能履行如实告知义务，或者对某些重要事实有所隐瞒，弄虚作假时，保险公司可以宣布保险合同无效，对被保险人提出的索赔可以拒赔。

7.5 保险市场

保险市场是保险交易产生的场所，也是保险各参与方参与到保险合同中产生相互作用和联系的一个有机整体。

保险市场上有两个主要的参与主体：保险产品提供者与保险产品需求

者。大部分的保险产品是由保险公司提供。保险单可以由保单所有人或者政府机构所持有。最近几年来，很多商业银行纷纷建立了自己的保险公司，希望能够打入这个正在成长的保险市场中。同时，个人、家庭、商业企业、团体组织和政府机构都会选择购买保险。

保险产品的销售方式有两种：直接销售渠道，即由保险公司直接向潜在客户群销售保险产品；间接销售渠道，即由保险经纪人或保险代理人来销售保险产品。投保人必须向保险公司支付保险费。保险公司收取保险费的目的是为了未来对实际损失进行偿付。保险公司通过计算风险发生的概率以及风险发生时损失的程度，从而计算出其应该收取的合理的保险费数额。

对于投保人来说，购买保险主要产生于以下两种方式：主动购买或者保险公司推销。在双方第一次接触的过程中，保险公司的代表将主要致力于了解潜在客户的基本情况、需求和其购买保险的目的与动机。这个过程称为需求分析。主要就是对潜在客户及其家庭成员在遭受可能的风险时将会面临的主要困境是什么进行分析。有些风险是必须通过保险的方式来加以分散和管理的，而有些风险可以由受险人自留，这必须具体情况具体分析。接下来就是对潜在客户个人信息的基本分析与评价，然后再设定其保险方案的基本目标和目的。客户的个人理财目标是什么以及保险公司如何帮助客户去实现其个人梦想？通过以上分析，保险公司的代表将针对客户做出一个最佳的保险方案，以最大程度地满足客户的个人需求，保障客户的风险管理的安全性。在此次会见之后，保险公司代表将会拟出一份详细的个人保险建议书，包括如下内容：保险风险及保险责任，保险金额，所需要的保险品种和潜在客户的详细个人信息。如果保险公司代表是一个独立的保险经纪人，那么他可以将拟好的保险计划递交给不同的保险公司，从而争取要价最低。如果保险公司代表是某一特定保险公司的代理人，那么他将拟好的保险计划递交给代理的保险公司的承保部门。保险公司的承保部门将会对保险计划进行复审。如果保险公司认为该保险计划可行，可以承保，那么将会向上述代表报出自己的保险费标准。该代表将会将此通知给自己的客户。如果客户接受并且支付保险费，那么保险合同就正式生效。

Subject Topic(命题对话)

Dialogue One

(Joanna Wood is talking to David about the insurance of a product order.)

Joanna: Hi, this is Joanna Wood. I'm calling to discuss the level of insurance coverage you requested for your order.

David: I believe that we requested an amount twenty-five percent above the invoice value.

Joanna: Yes, that's right. We have no problem complying with your request, but we think that the amount is a bit excessive.

David: Yeah, but in the past, we've really been put in a bind because of damaged goods.

Joanna: I understand your concern. However, usual coverage for goods of this type is the total invoice amount plus only ten percent.

David: We could feel more comfortable, though, with twenty-five percent.

Joanna: Unfortunately, we will have to charge you extra if you want the increase in coverage.

David: But wasn't insurance included in the quote?

Joanna: That quote involved normal coverage. We can, however, arrange the extra coverage. But I suggest you contact your insurance agent there and compare rates.

David: OK. Thanks. I'll check it out. It may turn out to be cheaper on this end.

Dialogue Two

A: Good morning, sir. What can I do for you?

B: I'm leaving for Middle East next month. I will purchase insurance for the trip there.

A: Oh, you are talking of the personal Accident Insurance for those Going

Chapter 7 Insurance

Abroad. We have just introduced a program that is very fit for you.

B: What's the rate?

A: The daily rate is only 0.01%.

B: Do you have any requirement for the minimum insurance amount?

A: Yes, that's 5,000 yuan. How much would you like it to be?

B: 30,000 yuan. How much should I pay for the insurance if my trip is 30 days?

A: Just a moment, I'll work it out for you… It's 90 yuan.

B: The premium sounds reasonable. And what are the conditions?

A: Simply put, if you are injured or even die within the validity—of course,we hope such things never happen—we'll compensate for the loss.

B: Can I appoint two or more beneficiaries?

A: Sure. But you'd better specify what proportion you want each beneficiary to have.

B: How much will you pay if the insured dies?

A: As much as the insurance amount.

B: If is injured?

A: If depends on many factors. Here is a detailed brochure which lists indemnity arrangements as well as the risks, insurance conditions, insurance amounts and premium rates.

B: Let me have a close study of it… The terms and conditions seem acceptable. Will you write me a policy?

A: Yes, sir.

Questions and Answers(专业问答)

1.   Where was insurance originally applied to losses?

   —It was originally applied to losses at sea, where risks were great.

2.   What is the purpose of the insurance?

—Its purpose is to provide compensation for those who suffer from loss or damage.

3. What is the most important marine insurance in London?
—At the heart of the world's business in marine insurance is Lloyd's, a London corporation of insurers who issue most kinds of policies, but are especially active in marine insurance.

4. What does a contract of insurance refer to?
—It is one between a party who agrees to accept the risk(the insurer) and a party seeking protection from the risk(the insured).

5. What does "Householders Insurance" mean?
—It means that the insurance company offers the insurance for householders including fire, storms, riots, burst pipes, burglary, theft, and so on.

Exercises(练习)

Put the following phrases into English.

1. 损失补偿原则
2. 可保利益原则
3. 代位求偿原则
4. 风险共同基金
5. 最大诚信原则
6. 人寿保险
7. 人寿定期保险
8. 信用保险
9. 经济损失保险
10. 保护限额
11. 保险费评级

Chapter 7 Insurance

12. 保险中间人

13. 保险费率

14. 保险人无力偿债

15. 机会评估

16. 损失控制

17. 合同分保

18. 溢额再保险

19. 超额赔款

20. 损失赔付

Put the following sentences into Chinese.

1. In general, the "principle of indemnity" serves as a legal foundation for all parties to an insurance contract, the Insurance Company and the policyholder, so that in the event of a covered cause of loss, the policyholder will not recover more than the actual cash value of their loss.

2. The "principle of insurable interest" and the "principle of indemnity" support each other in that the insurance policy will only provide for indemnification of its policyholder as long as the insured entity suffers a financial loss or it's harmed, as a direct result of a covered cause of loss found within the insurance policy.

3. Most insurance policies permit the insurance company to recover the financial value of the loss to their insured policyholder, from a liable or negligent entity that caused the financial loss or harm to their insured policyholder.

4. An insurance contract determines the legal framework under which the features of an insurance policy are enforced.

5. Reinsurance is a means by which an insurance company (called the reinsured, ceding company or the direct insurer) shares the risk of loss with another insurance company (called the reinsurer).

179

6. With coinsurance, there is a contractual relationship between the policyholder and coinsurer, so that in the event of a loss each coinsurer is directly and separately responsible to the policyholder for paying its share of the loss.

7. An important part of underwriting is deciding what price to charge for the insurance, a process known as premium rating.

8. Insurers cannot pay all claims out of revenue received from premiums and investment income, because the timing of these payments and receipts cannot be coordinated; they must therefore maintain a fund that can be used to pay claims.

9. The intangible product is promises of satisfaction of prospective customers are asked to buy.

10. In a direct distribution channel, a sales person, called an agent or underwriter, contacts the ultimate consumer and reports directly to the insurer or to an intermediary, commonly called a general agent, who turn reports to the insurer.

Fill in the blanks with the following words.

Passage One

(before, basis, subject, occurred, states, available, adequacy, justified, position, fulfilled)

The principle of indemnity is the ____1____ of most short-term insurance contracts. This principle ____2____ that after a loss has ____3____, the insured shall as far as possible be placed in exactly the same financial position as he was ____4____ the loss occurred, subject to ____5____ of sum insured and all policy conditions and requirements being ____6____.

Certain policies are not ____7____ to the principle of indemnity, notably Personal Accident and Life policies with fixed sums insured. The modern approach of "reinstatement" and "new for old" covers put the insured in a better

Chapter 7 Insurance

financial __8__, but this is __9__ by the fact that second-hand replacement items may not be readily __10__.

Passage Two

(broad, depending, association, tailored, packages, policy, evaluate, vary, relevant, nature)

Before choosing an insurance __1__ you will need to __2__ your business's insurance needs. Your insurance requirements __3__ considerably __4__ on the type of business you operate.

Some insurers offer insurance package policies specially __5__ to cover your business needs. There are also individual products that may be __6__ to the particular __7__ of your business.

Your industry __8__ may also provide important insurance advice, some associations organize insurance __9__ for their members.

There are three __10__ types of business insurance: Assets & revenue insurance, People insurance and Liability insurance.

Passage Three

(consequences, view, scale, regulatory, convergence, affected, ever, imposed)

Insurance regulation is an issue of increasing interest on a global __1__. Regulation concerning __2__ globalization and multinationalization are important forces with real __3__ for insurers everywhere. But direct regulation of insurers by insurance regulators is arguably only one piece in the __4__ pie. Insurers around the world are increasingly __5__ by many policy and legislative decisions __6__ on them by noninsurance regulators. Securities regulators, monetary/fiscal policy authorities and even national security and military decisions are impacting insurance industry more than __7__. This presentation takes a broad __8__ of regulation, looking primarily at non-insurance regulatory and policy decisions that profoundly affect insurer operations.

181

Chapter 8

Securities

Securities are financial instruments, which not only realize the investment demand and fund raising demand, but also provide investors with a good investment tool.

8.1 The Types of Securities

8.1.1 Debt Securities

Debt securities are financial instruments that corporations and governments sell to the public to raise money for expanding their businesses, building new factories, developing mines, constructing airports, highways, railways, buying machinery and equipment. They are loans. The issuer borrows money from investors for a period of time—the term. The money is repaid periodically (monthly, quarterly, semi-annually, annually) or in one lump sum at maturity (the last day of the term).

An investor in debt securities earns a return in two ways:

1. By receiving regular interest payments (monthly, quarterly, semi-annually, annually) and/or;

2. By getting (either by selling in the market or redeeming at maturity) more money for the debt instrument than was paid for it.

Many debt instruments pay interest. The interest rate can be either fixed—does not change during the term of loans or floating—goes up and down as

Chapter 8　Securities

general interest rate levels go up and down.

Other debt instruments do not pay interest but are sold at a discount when they are issued—a price less than the face amount.

The main disadvantage of debt securities is that making the required interest payments and repaying the money borrowed at the agreed time in the future are legal obligations. If they are not paid, lenders have the right to take strong action including putting the company into bankruptcy.

8.1.2　Equity Securities

Shares, stocks, equities are words used to describe ownership of corporations. When we own shares in a corporation, we have the right to "share" along with all the other shareholders in the earnings of the business and in the net assets.

The main reason that a company would issue shares to the public is because:

1. it needs money to grow,

2. it cannot produce enough cash from its own operations and,

3. it would not be prudent to borrow more money (because of the risk of bankruptcy).

Investors buy shares for two reasons:

1. receive regular income (cash) in the form of dividends and,

2. earn capital gains—selling shares in the secondary market for more than was paid for them.

There are two main types of shares: preferred shares and common shares. Each type has particular rights and benefits, advantages and disadvantages.

Preferred shares are somewhat like bonds. They generally entitle the holder to receive fixed quarterly payments called dividends. There are two big differences, however, between bonds and preferred shares. Bond interest is paid first and then preferred dividends. Bond interest is a legal obligation of the

183

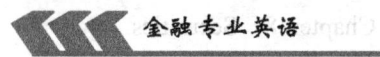

issuer. If it is not paid, bondholders can force the company into bankruptcy. While preferred shareholders expect to receive dividends, they have no legal right to force the company to pay them. If the company incurs a loss or is short of cash, it may not pay the expected dividends. The other difference relates to income taxes. Bond interest is paid before corporate income taxes are calculated whereas as dividends are paid out after tax income. Individuals pay income tax on interest they receive on bonds. The tax rate on dividends, however, is often lower to compensate for the double taxation—the same income being taxed twice, once when it is earned by the corporation and again when it is paid to the shareholders.

Common shares are at the very bottom of a company's capital structure. Common shareholders are entitled to whatever is left after all of the company's expenses such as wages, materials, interest and so on, have been paid and after preferred dividends have been provided for. Common shareholders are the most risky of the three types of investments we've been discussing—bonds, preferred shares and common shares—because they rank last. However, the potential rate of return is the highest because there is no upper limit on how high the price of the shares can rise.

8.1.3 Stocks

The success of the stock market is watched by millions of people worldwide. A bull market means profits for individuals and companies. A drop in the markets especially if the drop is great and sudden, can wipe out a person's life savings or ruin a company. Some people consider playing the stock market to be a form of gambling. Companies sell stock in their companies as a means of raising money to expand their business. The success of their stock is very important to the well-being of their company.

In western countries, corporations usually need a large amount of capital for the boost of their production and business, but their own funds are far from

Chapter 8   Securities

adequate. It is the stock issuance that makes it possible for them to fill up the gap.

The stocks are mainly issued through a special market in a very similar way to that of bond issuance. Buyers will obtain a kind of stock bills by providing their funds to the issuing corporation. But the relationship between a stock-issuer and its buyers is obviously different from that between a bond-issuer and its buyers. For a bond, it is establishing a debtor-creditor relationship between the issuer, who should pay on time the bond principal and interest, and the buyers, who will receive such repayment. But for a stock, it is an ownership certificate, which means that the buyer has become one of the members in possession of the issuer's properties and his share is equal to the face value of the stock he has purchased. In addition, there is no term for a stock, so in no circumstance can a buyer withdraw his investment from the stock except his reselling it in a secondary market or his claiming indemnity from the corporation when it is facing bankruptcy. What he can get annually is only the dividends and bonus drawn from the profit produced by the stock in which he has invested.

When a stock has been issued in the primary market and become negotiable for free purchase and resale in the secondary market, its price will depart from its original face value and fluctuate up and down along with the market tone. If there are more purchases than sales on it, which render its price up, it is called Bull Market; if on the contrary, it is called Bear Market.

Before their stocks appear in the primary market, most issuers will have them presented to authoritative institutions for appraising their credit standing grades, which will be often adjusted in line with their behaviors in the market later on.

Stocks, held by the buyers, may be in two forms. One is called Common Stock, that is suitable for all corporations because its holders will have the ownership of the corporation's profit and the interest produced by its assets, the right to vote for its board of directors and the right of asset distribution in case of

185

its bankruptcy. Another is called Preference Stock, which is adopted by part of corporations. Its holders will have the right to get a portion of dividends before its distribution to all Common Stock holders, but they have no right to vote or veto for the board of directors.

8.2　Securities Market

8.2.1　Stock Exchange

In China the stock exchange is now in general a non-profit-making legal entity with membership system. It is market which provides places for organized trading in securities, manages spot trading of listed stocks and bonds, supplies the customers with the services of securities clearing, delivery, transfer and storage, and with the market information. The exchange deals with other business activities or services permitted or entrusted by the People's Bank of China.

The securities listed in exchange include government bonds, corporation bonds, financial bonds and stocks publicly issued all over the country.

If you want to buy or sell securities in the market, you must entrust member company's broker to make the dealing, register for the roll and open a capital account and a securities account. Entrustment may include personal interview, contracts by telephone, telegraph, telex and letters. Entrustment price is divided into market price and limited price. The term of entrustment is divided into one-day and five-day validity.

In securities trading, only spot trading is allowed. The transaction includes the trading of one day, regular day and appointed day. The trading amount must be a set or its multiple. Brokers are organized to trade in stocks and bonds according to the principle of time priority and price priority. The delivery, settlement and ownership-transfer of the securities are carried out through the settlement department.

Chapter 8   Securities

8.2.2   NASDAQ

NASDAQ, acronym for the National Association of Securities Dealers Automated Quotation system, is one of the largest markets in the world for the trading of stocks. The number of companies listed on NASDAQ is more than that on any of the other stock exchanges in the United States, including the New York Stock Exchange (NYSE) and the American Stock Exchange (AMEX). The majority of companies listed on NASDAQ are smaller than most of those on the NYSE and AMEX. NASDAQ has become known as the home of new technology companies, particularly computer and computer-related businesses. Trading on NASDAQ is initiated by stock brokers acting on behalf of their clients. The brokers negotiate with market makers who concentrate on trading specific stocks to reach a price for the stock.

Unlike other stock exchanges, NASDAQ has no central location where trading takes place. Instead, its market makers are located all over the country and make trades by telephone and via the Internet. Because brokers and market makers trade stocks directly instead of on the floor of a stock exchange, NASDAQ is called an over-the-counter market. The term over-the-counter refers to the direct nature of the trading, as in a store where goods are handed over a counter.

Since its inception in 1971, the NASDAQ Stock Market has been the innovator. As the world's first electronic stock market, NASDAQ long ago set a precedent for technological trading innovation that is unrivaled. Now poised to become the world's first truly global market, the NASDAQ Stock Market is the market of choice for business industry leaders worldwide. By providing an efficient environment for raising capital NASDAQ has helped thousands of companies achieve their desired growth and successfully make the leap into public ownership.

187

8.3　Securities Investment

8.3.1　Stock Market Investment

Stock market investment gives you the unique opportunity to take a direct part in the growth and success of companies. When you buy shares in a company, it means that you actually own a portion of that company. As part owner, you benefit by receiving part of the profits or dividends and sharing in the growth of the value of the company.

The company benefits by raising funds or capital when your shares and other shares are first sold. These funds are used to operate and expand the business.

In general, share investments produce better returns than fixed interest investments, particularly when money is invested long term.

Although there are rises and falls in the stock market, history shows that over the long term, the value of the stock market rises. In the U.S., which has a long history of deregulated stock market, the average real return per annum after inflation is approximately 10%.

Direct investment in the stock market also gives you control over where you put your money. You decide which companies you want to invest in and when the time is right for you to see your shares. If you want to be in control, stock market investment is a good option.

Another attractive feature of stock market investment is the flexibility to change your investments when your personal circumstances change. For example, if you need money for a well-earned break, an extension on our house or your children's education, all you need to do is sell your shares.

Stock market investment allows you to follow your investment. You'll receive regular information from companies you invest in and can attend meetings. This enables you to gain a unique insight into the results and strategies

Chapter 8   Securities

of the organization and learn a lot in the process.

Stock market investment also allows you to follow a particular interest you have. For example, you may have lived all you life in a forestry area and are interested in supporting this industry and benefiting from its success, by investing in listed forestry stocks.

8.3.2   How to Pick a Stock?

When technical analysis is mentioned, people often think of analysts plotting price movements of stocks, drawing lines to find trends, support or resistance. Technical analysis is the art of deducing probable future trend from historical records of stock trading. It is the study of the stock market itself rather than the external factors that influence the market. The most familiar indicators used are the price and volume of a stock.

Advocates of technical analysis believe that information is not immediately reflected in the market prices of stocks. For example, when a piece of good news about a company is available, it is not immediately known to everyone but is slowly passed from one person to another. This process takes time and an upward price trend develops for that company as more and more people hear the good news and want to buy the stock and fewer and fewer people are willing to sell the stock. The stock price which has started to move in an uptrend will continue to do so until something happens to change the supply-demand balance.

For the technical analyst, he does not need to know what the good news or any other information that is affecting the stock price is; the chart will tell him whether the stock price is going to move up or down. He does not need to know the fundamentals of the company because if the price is going up, the fundamentals must be improving.

On the other hand, fundamental analysis examines all relevant factors affecting the stock price in order to determine an intrinsic value for that stock. If

189

the market price is below the intrinsic value, then the stock is undervalued and should be bought. The factors to consider include balance sheet items, corporate management, business prospects and earnings outlook. The fundamental analyst calculates financial ratios based on data available from the balance sheet and income statement of a company. From these ratios, he deduces the financial strength and earnings trend of the company. Then he will meet the company's management to affirm his deductions, to understand the business and to learn of any new development of the company and the industry.

A widely used tool in fundamental analysis is the price-earnings ratio or PE ratio. It is calculated using the stock price divided by the earnings per share (EPS) of a company. As a general rule, a stock with a low PE ratio is considered cheap although there are difficulties in applying this principle. PE ratios of two companies can only be compared if the companies are similar. It is believed that companies in different industries deserve different PE ratios. For example, Singapore Telecom is believed to deserve a higher PE ratio than many other stocks because of its position in the telecommunication business.

However, analysts have not yet agreed on what PE ratio each industry or company deserves and there is no one way to determine the right PE ratio. Both approaches attempt to predict the future price movement of a stock. Fundamentalists study the cause of market movement while technicians believe that the effect is all that they need to know. Despite their differences, both approaches try to increase your probability of picking up the right stock at a right price. However, these methods only increase your chances but do not guarantee complete success. Some believe that fundamental analysis is good for picking the right stock while technical analysis is appropriate to decide the right price or time to buy.

For the professional investor, he has to take another step of deciding the sequence of analysis. This will have an impact on how the investor divides his money among different countries and stocks. Basically, the investor decides whether the market as a whole or the company itself is more important in determining stock prices. Both factors definitely influence stock prices but the degree of influence is the issue.

The top-down approach or sometimes known as the Economy-Industry-Company (EIC) model emphasizes the market over the company. It starts with the analysis of different economies to determine which country could offer the investor better returns. In the selected economy, it searches for industries that provide better prospects and it picks the best companies within these industries. The top-down approach offers a systematic and structured way to analyze stocks. It advocates that the economy and industry effects are significant factors in determining the total return for stocks.

The bottom-up or stock picking approach believes in finding stocks that are undervalued which can provide superior returns irrespective of the market and industry factors. The company effect is the dominant factor in determining stock return.

There is no overwhelming evidence to suggest which approach offers superior returns to the investors. The most important thing is that an investor is comfortable with a particular method, understands its strengths and limitations, experiments with it, finds that it works for him and abides by the method.

参考译文

第8章 证券

证券是一个金融工具，它不仅能实现投资和筹资的愿望，也可以向投资者提供一个良好的投资工具。

8.1 证券的类型

8.1.1 债务型证券

债务型证券是一种金融工具，由企业和政府出售给公众以募集资金，用于扩张业务，修建新厂房，开发矿山，建设机场、公路、铁路，购买机器设备。债务型证券即贷款。发行者从投资者那里借用一段时间(期限)资金。资金通常会定期(每月，每季，每半年，每年)偿还，或在到期日一次性偿还总金额。

债务型证券投资者有两种赚取回报的方式：

(1) 定期收到利息(每月，每季，每半年，每年)和/或；

(2) 获得比当初支付还要多的一笔资金(通过市场销售或到期赎回的方式)。

许多债务型证券都支付利息。利率可能固定不变(在贷款期限内不变)，也可能是浮动的(随市场一般利率水平上下浮动)。

其他一些债务工具不支付利息，但是在发行时折价销售(价格低于面值)。

债务型证券的主要缺点是，在约定时间内按时偿还本金和所需支付的利息是法律义务。如果到期不支付，贷款人有权采取强有力的行动，包括令公司破产。

8.1.2 权益型证券

shares、stocks 和 equities 都是用来描述企业所有权的词汇。当我们拥有一个公司的股份时，我们就有权利与所有其他股东一起"分享"企业收益和净资产。

公司向公众发行股票的主要原因如下。

(1) 需要资金来发展。

(2) 经营中难以产生足够的现金。

(3) 不愿借更多的钱(因为破产风险的存在)。

投资者购买股票的原因有两个。

(1) 以股息形式获得定期收入(现金)。

(2) 赚取资本利得——在二级市场上以高于买价的价格出售股票。

股票主要有两种类型：优先股和普通股。每个类型都有特定的权利和利益，并各有优缺点。

优先股有点类似于债券。优先股持有人有权得到固定的按季度支付的分红，即股息。不过，债券和优先股之间还是有两大区别。债券利息支付在前，优先股股息支付在后。债券利息是发行人必须履行的法律义务。如果不支付，债券持有人可以迫使该公司破产。而优先股股东尽管期望得到红利，他们却没有合法权利迫使公司支付。如果公司亏损或现金短缺，就可能无法支付预期股息。另一项差异涉及所得税。债券利息在计算企业所得税之前支付，而股息是在税后支付。个人获得债券利息需缴纳个人所得税。而股息的税率往往较低，以补偿双重征税，即同样的收入征税两次，一次对上市公司，第二次对股东。

普通股在公司资本结构的最底层。普通股股东有权获得剩余部分，即支付了公司所有开支(如工资、原材料费用和利息等)，以及支付优先股股息以后剩余的可供分配的资产。普通股是我们正讨论的三类投资(债券、优先股和普通股)中风险最高的证券，因为它排名最后。然而，普通股的潜在回报率也是最高的，因为股票价格上涨的高度没有上限。

8.1.3　股票

全世界千百万人都在注视着股票市场的成功。牛市意味着许多个人和公司将能获利；市场的下跌，特别是突然的大幅下跌，则可能耗尽一个人毕生的积蓄或毁掉一个公司。有些人认为"炒股票"是一种赌博。公司出售股票以便筹集资金以扩大经营，确保股票的成功对公司的利益是极其重要的。

在西方国家，公司为扩大其生产经营而需要筹集的资金单靠自身财力状况往往不能承受，所以发行股票是弥补其资金缺口的方法之一。

股票主要是通过专门市场发行，这与发行债券的方法相似。购买股票的人是向公司，即股票发行者提供资金以取得股票。但股票发行人和购买者的关系却与债券发行人和购买者的关系明显不同。债券使发行人和购买人之间形成债务人和债权人的关系。债务人须按期向债权人支付本金和利息。而股票则是一种所有权凭证，证明股票购买人已成为拥有公司财产的一分子，其占有份额与其出资购买的股票面值相等。此外，股票是无期限的，因此股票购买人不能半途退股要回资金，除非他将股票在二级市场上转卖，或者在企业濒临倒闭时向公司提出索偿要求。他每年只能从所投资的股票产生的利润中收取股息和红利。

股票在初级市场发行和在二级市场自由买卖后，其价格就将脱离原票面价格而随市场行情上下波动。如某一种股票买入多于卖出，从而使其价格上升，就称为"牛市"，如果情况相反，则称为"熊市"。

在股票上市前，多数股票发行人要请权威性评估机构进行资信级别的评估。上市以后，股票的等级也要按其表现不断进行调整。

持股人手中的股票一般分为两种形式。一种叫"普通股"，适用于所有公司。其特征是，持股人对企业利润和资产所产生的利息有占有权，享有对股份公司董事会的选举权和公司破产后资产处理的分配权。另一种叫"优先股"，为部分公司所采用。持有这种股票的人，在对普通股持有人分配股息之前，享有先获得部分股息的权利，但他们对董事会无选举权和否决权。

8.2 证券市场

8.2.1 股票交易所

中国目前的股票交易所通常是会员制、非营利性的法人组织。它是专门为办理股票交易、管理上市股票和债券的现货交易提供场所，为客户提供证券的清算、交割、过户和保管以及市场信息的市场。股票交易所还经办其他业务活动，或者经中国人民银行许可或委托的业务活动。

在交易所挂牌上市的有价证券包括在全国公开发行的政府债券、公司债券、金融债券和股票。

如果有人想在市场上买卖证券，必须委托会员公司的经纪人才能进行交易，进行名册登记，开立资金账户和证券交易账户。委托手续包括私人会见，通过电话、电报、电传和信函订立合约。委任价格分为市场价格和限制价格；委托期限分为当日有效和五日有效。

证券买卖只允许现货交易，交易类别分为当日交易、普通日交易和定日交易；交易金额为一个交易单位或其倍数。经纪人按照时间优先原则和价格优先原则，有组织地进行股票和债券的买卖；证券的交割、结算、过户则通过结算部门进行。

8.2.2 纳斯达克

纳斯达克(NASDAQ)是全美证券交易协会自动报价系统的首字母缩略词。它是当今世界上最大的股票交易市场之一。纳斯达克名下的上市公司在数量上超过了包括纽约证券交易所和美国证券交易所)在内的任何一家美国证券交易所。与纽约证券交易所和美国证券交易所的多数上市公司相比，在纳斯达克上市的大多数公司规模较小。纳斯达克已经成为新技术公司——尤其是计算机和与计算机相关的行业——的基地。纳斯达克的交易是通过代表客户利益的股票经纪人发起的。这些经纪人与专注特定股票买卖的市场期票出票人进行协商以确定股票的价格。

与其他证券交易有所不同，纳斯达克没有股票交易的中心交易场所。它的市场期票出票人遍及全美各地，通过电话和国际互联网进行交易。由于股票交易是由经纪人和市场期票出票人直接进行，而不是在股票交易大厅内进行的，因此，纳斯达克被称为买卖双方直接交易市场。该术语指出了其交易的直接性质，就如同在商店柜台直接进行商品的买卖一样。

自 1971 年诞生之日起，纳斯达克股票市场就成了产业的革新者。作为世界上第一家电子股票交易市场，纳斯达克早就史无前例地进行了技术交易的创新。现在纳斯达克已稳稳地成为世界第一家真正意义上的全球股票交易市场，是全球产业界领袖的首选市场。通过提供一个有效的融资环境，纳斯达克已经帮助成百上千家公司完成了其市值的预期增长，同时也成功地、跨越式地实现了公司股权的公众所有。

8.3　证券投资

8.3.1　股市投资

股市投资给你一个独一无二的直接参与公司发展的机会。当你购买了某个公司的股票，也就意味着你实际上拥有了公司的一部分。作为公司的部分拥有者，你有权分享公司发展所带来的利润或者红利和公司发展所带来的增值。

公司通过发行股票募集资金或资本获利。当你或他人购买了公司新发行的股票，公司也就募得了资金，用于公司的运营和业务拓展。

总体来说，股票投资比固定利率投资的回报率要高，尤其是在长期投资方面更是如此。

虽然股市有涨有跌，但历史证明，从长期来看，股市呈上升趋势。美国股市历来不受什么管制，其年均回报率，扣除通货膨胀率以后为 10% 左右。

直接投资于股市让你可以把握投资去向。你可以自己决定投资于哪家公司，何时卖出股票。如果你想对投资有所把握，股市是一个不错的选择。

Chapter 8 Securities

股市投资另一个吸引人的地方就是它的灵活性。你可以根据自身情况的变化而改变投资。比如说当你想去度假、扩建房子或者为孩子的教育而需要用钱的时候，你要做的就是卖出股票。

股市投资让你可以跟踪投资去向。你可以从所投资的公司定期得到信息，还可以出席公司的会议。这将使你更加深入地了解到公司的发展战略和进程，从中你也会学到很多东西。

你还可以按照各人爱好进行投资。比如，你一辈子都住在林区，你也想支持林业的发展，就可以投资上市的林业公司，你还可以从公司的发展中获益。

8.3.2 如何选择股票？

一提起技术分析，人们就会想到股票分析员画股价走势图，找支持线和阻力线。基本上，这个方式是根据过去的记录预测未来表现。换句话说，技术分析研究股市本身，不是影响它的外在因素，而股价和成交量是它最常用的数据。

技术分析的支持者认为，影响股价的消息没有立即反映在股价上。举例说，一家公司的好消息并不是每个人都同时知道，而是从一人传到另一人，整个过程需要一段时间。越来越多人知道这好消息后会买进，而越来越少的人愿意卖掉，这么一来使股价逐步升高。股价会因此继续上升直到供应与需求的平衡出现变化。

但对技术分析员来说，他并不需要知道那好消息是什么，走势图将告诉他股价会起还是落。他也不需要知道公司的基础因素，对他来说，基础会随着股价上升而改善。

另一方面，基础分析则研究所有可能影响股价的因素，以确定股票的实际价值。如果市价低过实值，就值得买进。基础分析员研究资产与负债表的项目、企业管理层、业务展望和盈利潜能，再根据资产与负债表和损益表提供的数据计算而得的比例，判断这家公司的财力和盈利趋势。分析员也会与公司的管理层会面，了解它的业务以及有关公司和行业的最新发展。

金融专业英语

本益比是基础分析中最常用的比例，计算方式是股价除以每股盈利。一般来说，低本益比表示股票便宜。不过，这个准则有时不太好用。两家公司从事相同的业务，才能够比较它们的本益比；不同行业的公司，本益比通常是不一样的。举例说，以新加坡电信在电信业的地位，它的本益比会较其他公司高。

对于每个行业的本益比应是多少，分析员们到目前为止还没有定论，而且也没有计算正确本益比的方式。技术分析和基础分析都尝试预测股价今后的走势。基础分析员研究市场走向的起因，而技术分析员只分析结果。它们的做法虽然不一样，但都尽可能帮助投资者以合适的价格买入有增值潜能的股票。不过，它们都只能提高可能性，而不能保证成功。有些人认为，基础分析较适合用于选择股票，而技术分析则适用于决定买入的时机和价格。

对专业投资者来说，他们还必须决定分析的步骤。这将影响投资者把资金分配于不同市场和股票的决定。基本上，他们要判断是市场的整体走势还是公司本身对股价的影响比较大。这两个因素都会影响股价，但程度可能不同。

从上至下的方法(也称 EIC 模型)侧重于整体市场。它首先决定哪个市场能带来较高的回报，然后再选择具投资展望的行业和属于这一行业的公司。这是个系统化的股票分析方式，认为经济和行业是决定股票回报的重要因素。

而从下至上的选择股票方式，无视市场和行业因素，重点是选择市值低于股值的股票，认为公司本身是决定回报的最重要因素。

哪个方式能带来较高的回报，并没任何研究证明。最重要的是投资者懂得所选择方式的优缺点，并尝试使用，证明它适合自己后就可沿用该方式。

198

Chapter 8   Securities

Subject Topic(命题对话)

Dialogue One

Here is the dialogue between Kirk(K) and Peter(P) about how to finance.

K: Thanks for coming over, Peter. I'm sorry I couldn't go to your office today.

P: That's all right. It's not unusual for a stockbroker to keep these hours. And besides, you're an old friend.

K: Have a seat. Let's start by having some coffee.

P: Fine.

K: So, as I was saying, Peter. I think this might be a good time for me to invest in that computer company. As my stockbroker, what do you think?

P: I think they're doing extremely well. And they would probably welcome your investment.

K: If they're doing so well, why do they need my investment?

P: All right. Let me explain a little about corporate finance.

K: Go ahead. When it concerns my money, I'm very interested.

P: First of all, corporate enterprises need financing, especially if they want to expand. Now, there are two basic types of financing.

K: And what are they?

P: Equity and debt.

K: What's the difference?

P: The use of money supplied by the owners of a business is called equity funding, and the use of money supplied by loans is called debt funding.

K: So what am I, as an investor?

P: Well. You become a partial owner of the company and receive equity. You get shares or certificates of common stock to represent your portion of ownership.

199

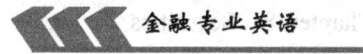

K: That's where you come in, right? Buying the stock for me.

P: Right. By the way, I brought a copy of the company's Annual Report over for you to look over. You should read it very carefully. Ask me if you have any questions about anything in it.

K: Thanks, Peter, I will. Say, does this company pay dividends on its stock?

P: Yes. As a matter of fact, I've looked into this organization very carefully. I can report that they have good management, their business is doing quite well and the value of their stock has been rising. I consider this to be an excellent long-term investment.

K: But suppose I want to sell my shares soon?

P: No problem. You should no doubt make a profit on the sale. But I think you might want to keep this company in your portfolio.

K: I must say that you've always given me good advice.

P: Well, my advice now is to study the company's Annual Report. You need several days to do that. Then we'll talk some more.

Dialogue Two

Here is the dialogue between Henry Hunter(H) and Robert Williams(R) on stock investment.

H: Hello, Mr. Williams. It's good to meet you. Have a seat, please.

R: Thank you. As you may know, I wanted some advice on how to invest my money. I have almost no experience with investments and I feel I don't have enough knowledge or information to make intelligent choices. One of your clients, a Mr. John Roosevelt, recommended that I see you.

H: Well, I can understand your concern. There are many investment possibilities, and conditions fluctuate so much nowadays.

R: The first area I thought about was stock. My wife and I have a few shares in utility companies already, so stocks are not completely strange to me.

H: I should tell you that there are two ways to look at investing in stocks. First,

Chapter 8　Securities

there are long-term investments. You can put your money into stable companies with a relatively secure yield. Or, you can concentrate on buying stocks that promise a good, rapid growth rate and resell them at a profit.

R: Well, I guess the second option means that I'd have to watch the stock market pretty carefully. I know I don't have time for that.

H: You're right. Your investment strategies would depend on whether you were facing a bullish or bearish market. You'd also have to consider factors in the economy such as a slowdown or a recession, double-digit inflation, interest rates, and other things that affect the companies you invest in.

R: I'd like to know what kind of stocks you've been recommending. Which sectors of the economy have been strong lately? What are the areas I ought to think about?

H: Well, we've had some good results with high-yielding bank shares recently, and experts are predicting these will appreciate quickly in the near future. The network companies have been doing well and high technology stocks have also had high earnings.

R: I've read that the market has been pretty bearish lately. It must be a good time for bargain-hunters to invest.

H: True, but bargain-hunters mustn't just buy stocks unless they make sure that the companies they invest in can maintain their growth through difficult times. Otherwise those investors may be faced with declining values.

R: Well, you've given me some valuable information. Let me talk things over with my wife and I'll talk to you again next week.

H: Good. Let's see if we can make some money for you then.

Questions and Answers(专业问答)

　　1.　　How do you understand debt securities ?

—Debt securities are financial instruments that corporations and governments sell to the public to raise money.

2. What are the reasons for a company to issue stocks?

—It needs money to grow and cannot produce enough cash from its own operations. And it would not be prudent to borrow more money.

3. How do you define that two forms of stocks?

—There are two forms of stock. One is called Common Stock, that is suitable for all corporations because its holders will have the ownership of the corporation's profit and the interest produced by its assets, the right to vote for its board of directors and the right of asset distribution in case of its bankruptcy. Another is called Preference Stock, which is adopted by part of corporations. Its holders will have the right to get a portion of dividends before its distribution to all Common Stock holders, but they have no right to vote or veto for the board of directors.

4. What does "NASDAQ" stand for ?

—The short form of NASDAQ is for the National Association of Securities Dealers Automated Quotation.

5. What securities can be traded in the market?

—The securities listed in exchange include government bonds, corporation bonds, financial bonds and stocks publicly issued all over the country.

Exercises(练习)

Translate the following terms into Chinese or English.

1. 股票上市公司

Chapter 8　Securities

2. 市盈率

3. 股本

4. 认购

5. 包销商

6. share incentive mechanism

7. market capitalization

8. Initial Public Offering(IPO)

9. retail

10. blue chip

Translate the following sentences into English or Chinese.

1. 股息是一家公司或基金给投资者的收入分配。公司可以用现金或股票的形式支付股息，虽然公司并没有义务给它的普通股股东分红。可是，公司通常会对优先股发放固定的股息。优先股股东并不确定会收到固定的优先股股息，他们可能收到累积股息或非累积股息。当董事会决定支付股息时，通常按照季度和股东所持有的股份分红。

2. A-share and B-share prices closed sharply higher in heavy trade, as retail investors carried out strong buying in response to further indications that the government is launching a major program apparently aimed at ramping up share prices, dealers said. The Shanghai A-share index closed 150.77 points or 9.2 percent　higher at 1,781.79 on turnover of 47.83 billion yuan, while the B-share index closed 13.70 points or 9.7 percent higher at 155.44 on turnover of 648.08 million US dollar.

Please simulate a dialogue between a broker and an investor in the trading of stock with your partner.

203

Part III Financial

Communications

- Chapter 9   Banking Communications on Remittance
              and Collections
- Chapter 10   Banking Communications on Letter of Credit
- Chapter 11   Correspondent Banking
- Chapter 12   Credit Inquiry

Chapter 9
Banking Communications
on Remittance and Collections

9.1 Mail Transfer

Mail Transfer(信汇)是汇出行应汇款人的要求，将付款指示以邮寄的方式转递给汇入行。下面是汇入行写给汇出行的电函，电函中说明因汇出行在信汇委托书上漏写了受益人的账号，故无法解付此款。

Re: Your Mail Transfer dated March 10, 2005

With reference to your captioned mail transfer, we regret to inform you that we are unable to effect payment due to the absence of the account number of the beneficiary in the mail transfer given. Therefore, we shall appreciate it if you will make us informed about it as soon as possible.

We look forward to your early reply.

9.2 Demand Draft

Demand Draft(票汇)指的是汇出行应汇款人的申请，代汇款人开立银行汇票，并由汇款人交给收款人，最后通过银行办理托收或直接解付票据款项。下列电函是有关出票行，即汇款行对丢失票据的止付通知。

Re: Our Draft No. 12345

In respect of our draft No.12345 which was reported missing, we wish to advise you that our New York Office has placed "stop payment" to the above-mentioned draft as requested.

If you want the amount of the draft to be paid by our New Your Office, you may approach them direct with a Banker's Letter of Indemnity acceptable to them.

9.3 Telegraphic Transfer

Telegraphic Transfer(电汇)是汇出行应汇款人的申请，通过 SWIFT 指示和授权汇入行解付一定金额给收款人的汇款方式。

Re: Your Telegraphic Transfer on May 5, 2006

With reference to your captioned telegraphic transfer, we find that there is no account number of the beneficiary. Please look at the matter and make us informed the result.

9.4 Accounts Intercourse

账户往来分为银行之间和银行与客户之间两种情况。

(1) 银行帮助客户办理销户并转移资金的电函。

Re: Transfer of Gray's Account # AO 1234

Enclosed are savings passbook # AO1234 and customer's draft # B 5678 in the name of Sam Gray. Please close the account and forward the principal balance plus any accrued interest to OVERSEAS CHINESE BANK CORP., LTD. A postage paid envelope is enclosed for your convenience.

Chapter 9 Banking Communications on Remittance and Collections

We thank you for your assistance in this matter.

(2) 银行通知客户关闭支票账户。

Re: Your Unused Cheques Nos. 33478
& 33479 for Closing Your A/C

According to our regulations, our customers should return all the unutilized blank cheques to us for cancellation before closing their checking accounts in our books. We shall appreciate it if you will send back to us the unused cheques in connection with your account No. 33671 so that we can remit the balance to your account with ABC Bank, New York.

We thank you for your cooperation.

(3) 银行通知客户账户透支并帮助客户申请信用额度。

Re: Your Account 12345 Overdrawn

The amount of your account overdrawn at close of business yesterday was USD2000 and it will be appreciated if you could arrange for credits necessary to clear this balance as soon as possible. Overdrafts are allowed to customers only by previous arrangement, and we notice that your account runs on a very small balance. You may need to come to some arrangement for overdraft facilities. If so, please bring with you details of the contracts you mentioned and also a copy of your last audited balance sheet next week, and we can then go more fully into the question of overdraft facilities.

(4) 请求在对方银行开立一个人民币账户。

Re: Opening a Renminbi Account

In recent months, we have been asked to open an increasing number of letter of credit denominated in Renminbi by our clients.

In this regard, we feel that rather than asking you draw in USD on our New

York correspondent in reimbursement of each negotiation, it may be simple for us to open a Renminbi account with you and to give you the authority to fund the account by drawing on the FIRST SAUDI BANK, New York in certain amount of US currency when funds are required. Negotiations under our Renminbi letter of credit can then be debited to the account in your books.

If you deem this arrangement acceptable to you, we will give you the necessary authority to draw on the said FIRST SAUDI BANK, New York, whom we shall authorize to honor your drawings.

We anticipate to receive your early favorable reply.

(5) 有关我们银行账户(12345)的对账单。

Re: Statement of Our A/C No. 12345

As your statement of our captioned account ending November 30 does not indicate particulars for the amount US$7,360 and US$6,830 of November 17 and 23 respectively on the debit side, we are not able to trace them in our records.

We shall be much obliged if you will advise us of nature of these transactions and our reference number so that we can do the needful on our part.

(6) 有关我们金额为 100 000 美元的借记通知(56789)。

Re: Our Debit Advice No. 56789
For USD100,000

With reference to the captioned debit advice claiming cable charges from you through City Bank, we regret to state that owing to an oversight on our part the above claim was lodged on you by mistake. Now that City Bank has reversed the entry at our request, you may consider our said debit advise as null and void.

We apologize for inconvenience you might have been caused in the matter.

Chapter 9　Banking Communications on Remittance and Collections

9.5　Letters on Collections

Sample 1

Your Collection No. 3456-02

We are in receipt of your captioned collection along with the relative documents, which have been duly forwarded to the drawees.

In this connection, we have been today informed by our clients that they disagree to make payment for the reason that the bill of lading under the collection bears "tank at one end slightly rusty outside." They will, however, effect payment upon arrival of the goods according to their actual condition.

Sample 2

Coll. No. 56708 dated May 2, 2003

Our client, G&T Co., Ltd., asks you to change the drawees of the captioned collection to BB Chemicals In., New York. We accordingly enclose herewith the new documents made out in the name of the new drawees.

Draft—in duplicate

Invoice—in triplicate

Weight List—in triplicate

Inspection Cert.—in duplicate

Please return to us at your earliest convenience the documents previously sent to you.

We look forward to you early attention to this matter.

Sample 3

Return of Document under
Our Coll. No. OC-03-6781

We thank you for returning the unpaid documents under the captioned collection along with your letter dated June 23, 2003 which have been duly notified to the drawers.

To close this item, please arrange with the payers to return, at our expense, the relative parcel to the drawers under their advice to us. As instructed, we have today remitted your handing charges of USD116. 500 to Bank of China, Hong Kong for your account.

We appreciate your kind assistance and look forward to your reply.

Sample 4

<u>Payment of Your Coll. No. 223372</u>

<u>Through ABC Bank</u>

Referring to your enquiry dated May 21, 2003, we have the pleasure of informing you that the said collection was already paid and the proceeds were remitted to your account with Credit Lyonnais in Paris on June 13, 2003.

Enclosed is a copy of our relative payment order for your reference. We consider this item as closed now. Please approach the above bank direct, if you still cannot trace receipt of payment.

We expect further cooperation with you in the future.

Sample 5

<u>Our Documentary Collection No. DC5348</u>

<u>for USD7,430.00 Drawn by P&T Co., Hong Kong</u>

We wish to draw your attention to the fact that this collection remains outstanding in our records. You are requested to investigate the matter and inform us of the present status of this item.

If you have already sent report to us, which should reach us after the date of this tracer, please disregard this request.

We thank you in advance for your cooperation in this matter.

Chapter 10

Banking Communications

on Letter of Credit

10.1 Letters between Banks

Sample 1

Our T/T Claim for USD15,960.00

under Your L/C No. 37086-T-63

Reference is made to the credit advice No. R-45368 from our New York Office in settlement of the above claim. We have found that our account has been credited with a USD15,510.00 which is USD450 less than our claim.

We would request you to kindly look into the matter and pay the difference of the said USD450 to our account under advice to us.

We thank you for your kind cooperation in this regard.

Sample 2

Our BP No. 402471 For USD73,450

Under Your L/C No. 14-3165

We acknowledge receipt of your Credit Advice under the captioned item. However, upon checking it, we found a difference between the amount of your credit advice and the amount of our payment as shown below:

Amount of your Credit Advice: USD71,450

Amount of our payment: USD73,450

We shall very much appreciate it if you will look into your records and give us any information on how the difference came about.

We anticipate to receive your early reply.

Sample 3

<u>Your L/C No. T-93401 for DM35, 705.00</u>
<u>in Favour of BBB Shoes Factory, Guangzhou</u>

We have received your captioned L/C and delivered it to the beneficiary today.

We, however, should like to point out that, the description of the merchandise stated in the L/C indicates that an import licence is an integral part of the credit. We did not find it enclosed.

Kindly look into the matter and rush it to us, unless you have dispatched one to us before your receipt of this letter.

10.2　Letters on Credit Operations

信用证通知行在收到开证行发来的信用证后，会立即准备一份信用证通知函给受益人。

(1) 信用证通知书。

① We enclosed herewith the original and one copy of the captioned Irrevocable Letter of Credit.

② We enclose the original of their Letter of Credit in your favor.

③ We confirm this credit and thereby undertake that all draft(s) drawn and presented as specified in the original credit will be duly honoured.

④ Dear Sirs,

We are pleased to acknowledge receipt of your:

Irrevocable Letter of Credit No. 123456

Issued on May 5, 2006

For the amount of USD60,000

In favour of the beneficiary: ABC Co.

And wish to inform you that as requested, we have delivered the original Credit to the beneficiary and have retained the duplicate in our file.

We thank you for your entrusting this business to us.

(2) 就受益人要求保兑信用证事，查询开证行可否照办。

The beneficiary of the captioned Letter of Credit has asked us to add our confirmation thereto.

Kindly inform us by airmail/cable as soon as possible whether we may comply with this request.

We await your reply and wish to assure you of our desire to be of your service at all times.

(3) 函告仅接到信用证修改书而未接到信用证正本。

Although we have informed the beneficiaries of this amendment on the strength of the duplicate, we have not received the original letter of credit. Thus we would request you to kindly investigate the matter and reply to us.

(4) 告来证漏打开证日期，请确认。

We thank you for the credit above which has just reached us. We find, however, that the date of issue of this credit does not seem to be indicated.

Will you please advise us of the date promptly.

(5) 更正原简电信用证上的到货港。

Enclosed herewith a clarification to the above-mentioned brief cable which shows "shipment from Hongkong to Shanghai" and "partial shipments not allowed".

We hereby confirm shipment should be "from Hongkong to Shenzhen" and "partial shipments allowed" as stated in this confirmation.

This confirmation is an independent instruction.

(6) 告信用证遗失。

We have been notified by the beneficiaries of the captioned credit that the original instrument of the credit, advised by us, has been lost. You are, therefore, hereby requested to mark your records and take due notice of not effecting negotiation against the original one.

In substitution for the lost credit, we have delivered them a verified copy which is marked: "This copy is intended to replace the original credit which has been declared lost".

Your kind attention to this matter will be deeply appreciated.

(7) 函告信用证编号有误。

We refer to your letter of amendment dated Feb. 12,1988 with the following text in confirmation of your cable of the same date:

CREDIT NO2151 SHIPMENT AND NEGOTIATION DATES EXTENDED TO 3/10/1988 and 13/11/1988 RESPECTIVELY.

In view of the fact that the credit number mentioned in your cable of Feb.15,1988 is 2115 and that the beneficiaries's name and the amendment are identical with those of your credit No. 2115, we have pass on the amendment to the beneficiaries taking 2115 as the correct credit number.

(8) 函告信用证修改书的受益人名称与原信用证不符。

It has come to attention that the beneficiary's name (address) as given in your letter of ... amending the subject credit differs from that mentioned in the original letter of credit.

We have, however, refrained from furnishing the beneficiary with notice of correction in this respect, as it appears to us that the beneficiary's name (address) as given in the original credit is correct.

Please inform us immediately if you have any objection in this respect.

(9) 信用证条款不全，可撤销还是不可撤销。

We wish to point out that the above letter of credit as received does not show whether the credit irrevocable or not.

Chapter 10 Banking Communications on Letter of Credit

Please, therefore, clarify this matter by return mail or, if you think it necessary, by cable.

To avoid delay, we have advised the beneficiary under reserve as per the enclosed copy of our advice.

(10) 信用证金额大小写不符，函请更正。

We wish to call you attention to the credit above which we have received from you and delivered to the beneficiary today.

The instrument shows the credit amount as ... in figures, whereas the credit amount spelt out read "...".

Your prompt clarification would be highly appreciated.

(11) 信用证常见的修改条款。

① Please add your confirmation to this Credit, confirmation charges, if any, are for account of buyer/seller.

② Shipment and validity extended to ... and ... respectively.

③ Beneficiary's name and address changed to read ... instead of previously advised.

④ Increase (decrease) credit amount by ... to ...

⑤ Please amend the price term to be on F.O.B. basis, freight to be paid by buyer.

⑥ Description of commodity changed to read "..." instead of previously advised.

⑦ Increase (decrease) the quantity of commodity by ... to ...

⑧ Shipment to be made per s/s "..."instead of "...".

⑨ Insurance covering marine risk ... instead of ...

⑩ Shipment to be made from ... to ... instead of original stated.

⑪ Partial shipment allowed.

⑫ Transhipment allowed.

⑬ This L/C is transferable.

⑭ All charges for this amendment including ours are for account of the

217

beneficiary, our charges USD20.00 will be deducted on payment against the credit.

⑮　Documents to be presented within 20 days after the date of issuance of shipping documents instead of previously stipulated.

⑯　B/Ls made out (to order of) ... instead of previously stipulated.

⑰　Delete the clause "...". The Clause: "..." deleted.

⑱　Insert the clause "...".

(12) 信用证转让通知书。

ADVICE OF TRANSFER OF COMMERCIAL CREDIT

To Messrs.

　　Re: Irrevocable Credit No.

　　　Issued by:

　　　In favour of

　　　For account of　　　　　　　　and/or transferee

Dear Sirs,

We are instructed by beneficiary(ies) of the above-mentioned Letter of Credit, under date of ... that the amount of ... has been transferred to you under the said credit, particulars of which are as per attached Photostat of the subject credit are letter of transfer.

This letter is to be attached when bills are presented. The amount of each bill negotiated under this Credit must be endorsed on the back hereof.

Please note that this letter is solely an advice and convey no engagement by us, and also note that any amendment to this advice shall be advised to you only upon, and in accordance with, the instructions which we receive from the original beneficiary(ies).

Kindly acknowledge receipt of this letter by signing and returning to us the attached copy of this letter.

Chapter 10　Banking Communications on Letter of Credit

(13) 应受益人要求撤销信用证。

We are in receipt of a letter dated MAY 15, 1989 from the beneficiaries returning the captioned L/C to us for cancellation.

A photo-copy of their said letter together with the original L/C and amendment(s) are enclosed herewith for your attention.

Chapter 11
Correspondent Banking

11.1 Terms and Conditions

寄送费率表

Re: Our Terms and Conditions

Thank you for your letter dated Jun. 10, 2005, the contents of which have received our prompt attention.

Now, we take pleasure to inform you that we have today sent our new Terms and Conditions which is to take effect on July 1, 2005.

I believe that you will see from our new Terms and Conditions that we have made certain adjustment to some items mostly relating telecommunication so as to offer more competitive rate to our clients.

We reassure you of our best services.

11.2 Signature Books and Test Keys

1. 签字样本的编号

Re: Your Signatures Nos. 3211 and 3212

L/C No. 88888

Upon comparing the caption two signatures appearing on the above credit with your Booklet in our possession, we are unable to verify them because now

Chapter 11　Correspondent Banking

we are only in possession of the specimens numbered 2378 as the maximum in your Booklet of Specimen Signatures. So authentication of the signature number 3212 is beyond possibility. Please look into the matter and let us know whether you have sent the above two specimen signatures, together with others to update the Booklet in our possession.

We anticipate your early attention to this matter.

2. 函开信用证上的签字

Re: Signatures on Your

L/C No. 12345 Dated June 10, 2005

Thank you for opening the above credit with us. We cannot, however, identify the signature thereon with your specimen signatures according to the number given.

As this credit involves a large amount, we cannot advise it to the beneficiary before receiving your confirmation by telex.

To complete our file, we would request you to send us your up-to-date supplements, if any, to your specimen signature book.

We thank you in advance for your early attention to this matter.

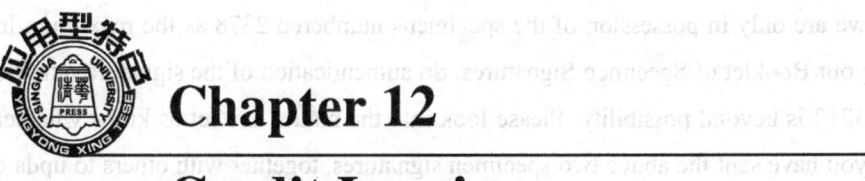

Chapter 12
Credit Inquiry

12.1 Credit Inquiry on Companies

客户要求贷款

Sample 1

Request for Information on ABC Co., Ltd.

ABC Co. in Australia wishes to obtain a generous amount of loan from us. You are cited as a reference. Please supply us with all the information with respect to the financial standing and the modes of business of the company, located on 11 Park Road, P.O. BOX 335, Sidney, Australia.

We assure you that the information you kindly give us will be treated as strictly confidential, and without any responsibility on your part.

We thank you in advance for your cooperation in this matter.

Sample 2

Request for Report on A & B Co., New York

A & B Company of New York wishes to have a large loan from us and has given you as a reference. We would be grateful if you would supply us with what information you can give about the company's general standing and whether, in your opinion, they are likely to be reliable for a credit line up to US$150,000, and whether they settle their accounts promptly.

We would be very glad to render you similar services should the need arise.

Chapter 12　Credit Inquiry

It is hardly necessary to add that any information you supply will be treated in strict confidence.

Your early attention to this matter is highly appreciated.

12.2　Credit Inquiry on Individuals

Sample 1

Request for Information on L & J Co., Hong Kong

We should be obliged if you could furnish us with a detailed report on the financial position, credit standing, business lines and general management of the captioned Company.

Any information sent to us will be held in strict confidence by us and will entail no obligation on your part.

We thank you very much for your assistance, and would be pleased to reciprocate your service any time in the future.

Sample 2

Private & Confidential

We shall appreciate your providing us with an opinion as to credit standing, respectability and financial responsibility of the following firm: East Trading Co., Ltd., Hong Kong.

Any information you give us will be strictly confidential. We shall, of course, be happy to reciprocate your courtesy whenever you allow us the opportunity to do so.

Key to Exercises

Part I Financial Markets

Chapter 1 Functions of Financial Markets

Reading Comprehension
Passage One: 1. A 2. B 3. C

Passage Two: 1. A 2. C 3. B

Passage Three: 1. A 2. D 3. A

Multiple Choice

1. C 2. A 3. B 4. A

Cloze Test

1. B 2. D 3. C 4. C 5. A

6. A 7. A 8. D 9. D 10. A

Chapter 2 Money Markets

Reading Comprehension
Passage One: 1. D 2. B 3. D 4. C 5. D

Chapter 3　Capital Markets

Reading Comprehension

Passage One: 1. D　2. C　3. C　4. A　5. B

Passage Two: 1. C　2. D　3. B　4. D　5. D

Passage Three: 1. D　2. B　3. B　4. D　5. A

Chapter 4　Foreign Exchange Markets

Reading Comprehension

Passage One: 1. B　2. D　3. C　4. A　5. B

Passage Two: 1. D　2. C　3. B　4. D　5. B

Part II　Financial Institutions and Their Operations

Chapter 5　Commercial Banking

Reading Comprehension

Passage One: 1. D　2. C　3. C　4. A　5. C

Passage Two: 1. B　2. B　3. D　4. C　5. B

Passage Three: 1. D　2. D　3. D　4. C　5. C

Passage Four: 1. D　2. A　3. D　4. B　5. D

Passage Five: 1. C　2. D　3. B　4. D　5. D

Put the following sentences into English.

1. Please remit the proceeds to the bank nominated in the Collection Order

225

after collection.

2. Banks have controlled over documents of title to goods before the importers effect payment.

3. With the development of international trade, some new methods of payment have been adopted.

4. A documentary letter of credit is a bank's credit instrument issued in favour of the exporter by an importer's bank at the request of the importer. It contains an undertaking that the issuing bank undertakes to honour the shipping documents presented by the beneficiary in case they are in full compliance with the credit terms.

5. If any bank cannot, for any reason, comply with the instructions given in the collection order received by it, it must immediately advise the party from whom it received the collection order.

6. Banks must verify that the documents received appear to be as listed in the collection order and must immediately advise the party from whom the collection order was received of any documents missing. Banks have no further obligation to examine the documents.

7. The presenting bank should endeavour to ascertain the reasons for such non-payment or non-acceptance and advise accordingly the bank from which the collection order was received.

8. Any charges and expenses incurred by banks in connection with any action for the protection of the goods will be for the account of the principal.

9. In the case of documents payable at tenor other than sight the presenting bank must, where acceptance is called for, make presentation for acceptance without delay, and where payment is called for, make presentation for payment not later than the appropriate maturity date.

10. When a bank handles a collection on behalf of a customer, two types of document may be handled: one is financial documents, the other is commercial documents.

Key to Exercises

11. We contacted the beneficiaries after receipt of your amendment and were told that they would accept it provided the validity could be further extended to May 31.

12. The beneficiary will not accept the credit unless it is confirmed by a third bank.

13. In letter of credit transactions, only the wording of the credits is binding on the relevant banks, not sales contracts.

True or False

1. T   2. F   3. T   4. T   5. F   6. T   7. F   8. T   9. F   10. F
11. F   12. T   13. T   14. F   15. F   16. F   17. T   18. T   19. T   20. T
21. T   22. F   23. T   24. F   25. T   26. T   27. F   28. F   29. T   30. F

Multiple Choice

1~10: A   D   D   D   B   C   D   C   B   A
11~20: B   A   D   B   D   A   B   C   C   A

Cloze Test

Passage One

1. safety   2. the overseas buyers   3. uniform   4. present
5. the issuing banks   6. meet

Passage Two

1. a financial document   2. having shipped   3. delivers   4. the buyer or importer   5. upon compliance with   6. against   7. over   8. default

Passage Three

1. C   2. A   3. D   4. B   5. A

Chapter 6   Investment Banking

Cloze Test

1. D   2. B   3. B   4. A   5. D

227

Chapter 7   Insurance

Put the following phrases into English.

1. principle of indemnity

2. principle of insurance interests

3. principle of subrogation

4. risk pool

5. principle of utmost good faith

6. life insurance

7. endowment life insurance

8. credit insurance

9. financial loss insurance

10. limits of protection

11. premium rating

12. insurance intermediaries

13. insurance rates

14. insurer insolvencies

15. opportunity assessment

16. loss control

17. treaty reinsurance

18. surplus share

19. excess of loss

20. loss settlement

Put the following sentences into Chinese.

1. 一般来说，对于一份保险合同的各方(即保险公司和保险单持有者)来说，"损失补偿原则"是一个法律基础，所以一旦发生了承保范围内的损失，保险单持有者获得的价值将不能超过损失的实际现金价值。

Key to Exercises

2. "可保利益原则"和"损失补偿原则"是互相支撑的，因为只要被保险的实体遭受了经济损失或受到的损失危害直接包含在保险单中，则保险人就会赔偿保险单持有者。

3. 大多数保险单允许保险公司从造成其保险单持有者经济损失或损害的实体处，弥补其保险单持有者的经济损失，只要该实体负有法律责任或玩忽职守。

4. 保险合同确定一个合法的框架，在这个框架下，执行保险单的特定条款。

5. 运用再保险的方式，一家保险公司(再被保险人、分出公司或直接保险人)可以同另一家保险公司(再保险人)分担风险的损失。

6. 在共同保险中，保险单持有者和共同保险人之间存在合约关系，因此，一旦发生损失，共同保险人都直接而单独地负责向保险单持有者支付其损失的份额。

7. 承保中，一个重要的部分是对保险的定价，也就是保险费评级。

8. 保险人不可能仅仅用保险费收入来支付索赔款，因为收入和支出的时间不可能协调一致。因此，必须维持一笔基金，用于支付索赔款。

9. 保险的无形产品就是保险人向潜在顾客承诺的满意度。

10. 在直接分销渠道中，一个销售人员，又称为代理人或承保人，与最终消费者联系，并直接向保险人或某中间商汇报，后者常称为总代理，也会向保险人汇报。

Fill in the blanks with the following words.

Passage One

1. basis   2. states   3. occurred   4. before   5. adequacy

6. fulfilled   7. subject   8. position   9. justified   10. available

Passage Two

1. policy   2. evaluate   3. vary   4. depending   5. tailored

6. relevant   7. nature   8. association   9. packages   10. broad

Passage Three

1. scale   2. convergence   3. consequences   4. regulatory

5. affected   6. imposed   7. ever   8. view

Chapter 8   Securities

Translate the following terms into Chinese or English.

1. public company

2. price/earnings ratio (P/E ratio)

3. share capital

4. subscription

5. underwriter

6. 股权激励机制

7. 市值

8. 首次公开招股

9. 散户

10. 蓝筹股

Translate the following sentences into English or Chinese.

1. Dividends are a distribution of earnings paid to investors by a company or a fund. Dividends may be paid in the form of cash or stock although a company is under no obligation to pay a dividend of any kind to its common shareholders. Preferred stock, however, is usually issued with the promise of a regular dividend. Depending upon whether the preferred stock is cumulative or non-cumulative, even preferred shareholders may not be sure of receiving dividend payments on a regular basis. When a board of directors does decide to pay a dividend, it usually pays it quarterly and according to the ownership interest of each shareholder.

2. 交易员称，国务院正式宣布暂停减持国有股后，散户积极入市，上海 A、B 股急升逾 9%，交投活跃。上海 A 股指数收市升 150.77 或 9.2%，报 1781.79，成交 478.3 亿人民币。上海 B 股指数升 13.70 或 9.7%，报 155.44，成交 6.4808 亿美元。

Please simulate a dialogue between a broker and an investor in the trading of stock with your partner.

Julia: Hello, can I speak to Mr. Smith?

Smith: Yes, speaking.

Julia: This is Julia speaking. I'd like to buy a stock.

Smith: What stock do you want to buy and how many?

Julia: I want to buy 1000 shares of Dubon.

Smith: Let me get the asking price of the stock. Just a moment. Oh, now the asking price is $80 each share. By the way, what is the offering price?

Julia: Let me see. The offering price is near or at $78.

Smith: Then the difference between the asking price and the offering price is $2. It's hard to take place today.

Julia: Do you mean that I have to buy at current price?

Smith: You can decide by yourself.

Julia: I heard that this stock would go up. Hmm, I will take it at current price.

Smith: So, now I will buy in. Are you sure?

Julia: Yes, please.

参 考 文 献

1. 陈建辉. 实用银行国际业务英语. 武汉：武汉大学出版社，2006
2. 金融英语教材编写委员会. 金融英语. 北京：清华大学出版社，2005
3. 金融专业英语证书考试委员会. 现代金融业务. 北京：中国金融出版社，2007
4. 李浚帆. 新编金融英语教程. 北京：清华大学出版社，北京：北京交通大学出版社，2008
5. 刘文国，蒋晓红. 金融英语. 第1版. 上海：复旦大学出版社，2006
6. 桑乃华. 金融英语业务知识综合训练. 北京：中国金融出版社，2005
7. 沈素萍，黄震华. 金融英语综合阅读. 上海：上海外语教育出版社，2009
8. 沈素萍，张红. 金融专业英语函电写作. 北京：对外经济贸易大学出版社，2006
9. 沈素萍. 金融英语阅读教程. 第2版. 北京：中国金融出版社，2006
10. 沈素萍. 金融专业英语阅读. 北京：对外经济贸易大学出版社，2006
11. 谢葆辉，蔡芳. 实用国际金融英语. 北京：电子工业出版社，2006
12. 沈素萍. 金融专业英语证书考试学习指导. 北京：中国金融出版社，2007
13. 金融专业英语考试委员会. 现代银行业务. 北京：中国金融出版社，2002
14. 顾雪帆，沈泽群. 国际金融实用英语教程. 上海：上海外语教育出版社，1993
15. 陈庆柏，王景仙. 金融英语信函与对话. 北京：世界图书出版社，2002
16. 张志辉. 金融保险英语口语. 北京：国防工业出版社，2004
17. 王垣，田力. 金融与保险专业英语. 哈尔滨：哈尔滨工程大学出版社，2004
18. 国际在线，www.crionline.cn
19. 西安教育信息网，www.029edu.com
20. 大耳朵英语网，www.ebigear.com